*C*TS

*Forthcoming Volumes in the New
Church's Teaching Series*

The Anglican Vision
James E. Griffiss

Opening the Bible
Roger Ferlo

Engaging the Word
Michael Johnston

The Practice of Prayer
Margaret Guenther

Living with History
Fredrica Harris Thompsett

Early Christian Traditions
Rebecca Lyman

Opening the Prayer Book
Jeffrey D. Lee

Mysteries of Faith
Mark McIntosh

The Christian Social Witness
Harold Lewis

Liturgical Prayer
Louis Weil

Ethics After Easter
Stephen Holmgren

Christian Wholeness
Martin L. Smith, SSJE

Engaging the Word

The New
Church's Teaching Series
Volume 3

Engaging
the Word

Michael Johnston

COWLEY PUBLICATIONS
Cambridge ✦ Boston
Massachusetts

The title *The Church's Teaching Series* is used by permission of the Domestic and Foreign Missionary Society. Use of the series title does not constitute the Society's endorsement of the content of the work.

Library of Congress Cataloging in Publication Data:
Johnston, Michael, 1946–
   Engaging the Word / Michael Johnston.
     p.   cm. — (The new church's teaching series; v. 3)
   Includes bibliographical references.
   ISBN: 1-56101-146-0 (alk. paper)
   1. Bible—Introductions. 2. Christian education—Textbooks for adults—Anglican. I. Title. II. Series.
BS475.2.J64 1998
220.6'1—dc21   97-51500
                                       CIP

Scripture quotations are from the *New Revised Standard Version* of the Bible, © 1989 by the Division of Christian Education of the National Council of the Churches of Christ in the USA. Used by permission. All rights reserved.

Editor: Cynthia Shattuck; Copyeditor and Designer: Vicki Black; Study Guide by Cynthia Shattuck.

Royalties from the sale of books in the New Church's Teaching Series have been donated to the *Anglican Theological Review*.

This book is printed on recycled, acid-free paper and was produced in Canada.
Second Printing
Cowley Publications
28 Temple Place • Boston, Massachusetts 02111
1-800-225-1534 • *http://www.cowley.org/~cowley*

Contents

The New Church's Teaching Series

Almost fifty years ago a series for the Episcopal Church called The Church's Teaching was launched with the publication of Robert Dentan's *The Holy Scriptures* in 1949. Again in the 1970s the church commissioned another teaching series for the next generation of Anglicans. Originally the series was part of an effort to give the growing postwar churches a sense of Anglican identity: what Anglicans share with the larger Christian community and what makes them distinctive within it. During that seemingly more tranquil era it may have been easier to reach a consensus and to speak authoritatively. Now, at the end of the twentieth century, consensus and authority are more difficult; there is considerably more diversity of belief and practice within the churches today, and more people than ever who have never been introduced to the church at all.

The books in this new teaching series for the Episcopal Church attempt to encourage and respond to the times—and to the challenges that will usher out the old century and bring in the new. This new series differs from the previous two in significant ways: it has no official status, claims no special authority, speaks in a personal voice, and comes not out of committees but from scholars and pastors meeting and talking informally together. It assumes a different readership: adults who are not "cradle Anglicans," but who come from other religious traditions or from no tradition at all, and who want to know what Anglicanism has to offer.

As the series editor I want to thank E. Allen Kelley, former president of Morehouse Publishing, for initially inviting me to bring together a group of teachers and pastors who could write with learning and conviction about their faith. I am grateful both to him and to Morehouse for participating in the early development of the series.

Since those initial conversations there have been substantial changes in the series itself, but its basic purpose has remained: to explore the themes of the Christian life through Holy Scripture, historical and contemporary theology, worship, spirituality, and social witness. It is our hope that all readers, Anglicans and otherwise, will find the books an aid in their continuing growth into Christ.

James E. Griffiss
Series Editor

Acknowledgments

The first debt this book owes is to my teachers. Not just the ones in the seminary classrooms, although they formally taught me first, but the whole range of what are known in the Greek as the *didaskaloi*, the masters—books I have read recently and long ago, sermons I have heard, lectures I have attended, papers and homilies of students I have pondered, prayers fashioned on all sorts of occasions, and even conversations over lunch. I have listened to all of you, and if the words and ideas of this book sound like yours, they probably are. I have tried to give credit in those places where I can clearly attribute credit. But I am primarily a preacher, and preachers, like poets, are notorious plagiarists. We think everything is the voice of the Holy Spirit, which speaks in the public domain.

The second debt is to my Bible students at St. Matthew's Church, Evanston, Illinois, and at the Church of the Epiphany in Chicago. It is from them that I have learned how to read Scripture within the life of the believing community. They have with great patience and good will listened to me as I have worked out, over the years, much of what follows in these pages. The vestry of St. Matthew's generously provided a sabbatical leave for the writing, and a number of study groups, both at St. Matthew's and at

Grace/St. Paul's Church in Mercerville, New Jersey, read the initial drafts of the manuscript so that I could "road test" the material with the kind of audience for which the book is intended.

The third debt is to a number of individuals who have read the manuscript, or parts of it, at various stages of development and offered many helpful suggestions: Roger Ferlo, Sharon Johnson, Sue Nebel, Timothy Sedgwick, and Ernest Vasseur. Suzanne Wagner was a tireless and loving editor of the first draft, and since then Cynthia Shattuck and Vicki Black of Cowley Publications have given the book its final shape.

Finally, I wish to express my fond appreciation to James Griffiss, who first suggested that I undertake this project and who has continued to support me along the way. The task he set has been a sacred one. As a "second career" priest, and an academic before ordination, I had yearned for exactly Jim's kind of invitation. To teach is in my blood, and to have been invited to write a teaching book about something as glorious as the Word is, for me, a blessed vocation, not really a task at all.

An Icon of the Word

The design for the cover of this book derives from an icon that was given to me by a friend when I got my first job as a parish priest. It sits on a shelf in my study, immediately above my computer, so I have spent literally hundreds of hours with it over the years. Crafting a sermon late on a Saturday night, drafting a note for a Sunday leaflet, or just writing a letter, I often stop and look up at its image. Sometimes I only rest my eyes on it while I untangle a twisted piece of prose knotted in my thoughts. Other times I ponder it anew, hoping to find some hint of the deep mystery that lies below its surface. So it is both a constant presence and a prayerful pause. The icon's figures are engaged in a writing project, and when they have not been otherwise occupied with their own work, they have looked down from time to time on the progress of mine. Thus it seems appropriate to begin this book about sacred Word with a word or two about this sacred image.

The icon's two human figures are named *Ho Hagios Johannes Ho Theologos* and *Ho Hagios Prochoros*—that is, Holy John the Theologian and Holy Prochoros. One of the reasons I am so fond of this icon is that I have been in love for a very long time with Holy John the Theologian and his holy book. I came first to Scripture by way of the Fourth Gospel.

Since my days in seminary Mark's gospel has risen enormously in my esteem, in part because I have learned to read its politics of liberation, so Mark competes now with John for my affections. But the truth is, I love them both. I do my politics out of Mark and I pray out of John.

It is sometimes difficult to identify who is who in icons, especially if the figures are local saints and unnamed, but there is no question about the identity of the pair in this one: the more venerable of the two is obviously Blessed John. He is also given away by his "signature," an eagle poised to take flight like the mystical words of John's gospel. The eagle clutches in its talons a book that looks as if it were bound in one of those elaborately decorated covers—sometimes gold or silver, and often studded with precious stones—used to contain the gospel books held high in processions and read or sung in the divine liturgy.

Blessed Prochoros, the evangelist's scribe, is taking dictation. I have not been able to track down precisely when he entered the iconographic tradition, but in the Bible a Prochoros is listed among the first seven deacons of the church, ordained with St. Stephen for daily service to the widowed and the poor. They were elected to tend to the practical tasks of caring for others so that the apostles might devote themselves more fully "to prayer and to serving the word" (Acts 6:4).

John and Prochoros lean toward one another, forming a circle of mutual intent. This posture has always struck me as a symbol of the discipleship community in general: sacred people assembled around the sacred task of proclamation. Still, each attends to his own individual business. Prochoros, like a good scribe, is listening with rapt attention to John while his gaze is directed toward the page on which he is writing. John looks away, however, perhaps trying to locate an idea in the regions of the abstract. But his gesture suggests that he has got it, and indeed he has. He has just uttered the opening line of the prologue to his gospel: "*En arche en ho logos*," "In the beginning was the Word." Those are the words written on the page in Prochoros' lap. Actually, the last word is unfinished; the line reads: "*En arche en ho logo*." The scribe's quill is rounding out the *o*, but we can assume that he is about to write the *s* of the Greek *logos*, which embraces an enormously complicated Greek theological idea. God is *Word* and was so at the beginning of time; God is *speech*; God *speaks* into history; and God *speaks* into humanity by the incarnation of his Word in Jesus the Christ. That the Logos has chosen to take on human flesh is, in fact, the essence of John's message of Good News.

For all the richness of its imagery, the single detail of this icon that has always intrigued me most is the set of five scrolls in the basket at Prochoros' right hand, neatly rolled and tied with a red cord. My guess is that those five scrolls are the Pentateuch, the first five books of the Hebrew Bible: Genesis, Exodus, Leviticus, Numbers, and Deuteronomy. From the perspective of Christian tradition, those texts are the writings of the old covenant, the old dispensation, which is the core of what we call the Old Testament. What we see Prochoros writing down here are the first words of the *new* dispensation, and it is not at all odd that the artist might place the old and new together. When you read those first five words that Prochoros is so carefully penning, you are meant to hear the first words of the book of Genesis: "*En arche ho theos*," "In the beginning God." Through John's deft choice of words, he makes a connection between old and new that would have fallen on his readers' ears with the same weight of authority that the phrase "As it is written" falls on ours. Thus does John seek to help his community make sense of its past in Judaism, order its present in Christ, and look toward its future in the life of the Holy Spirit.

My icon, then, is an image of the life of Holy Scripture in the life of a believing community, an image of the Bible as past, present, and future. The five scrolls are the roots of the John community in Judaism; the words *"En arche en ho logos"* are its reality in Christ; and the eagle is the soaring promise of its eternal life in the Holy Spirit. That is an icon of the Bible for us as well. Holy Scripture tells us where we have come from, who we are, and what we should be about.

Reading Scripture is a little like reading an icon. In fact, iconographers do not speak of "painting" but of "writing" an icon. So there are striking parallels between word and image as invitations into the divine life. When you pick up your Bible and thumb its pages, you are handling hundreds and hundreds of such invitations: on each page there is line, color, story, and movement of incredible richness and diversity. Sometimes when you pick up your Bible to read you will want simply to rest the eyes of your soul on its consoling images. Sometimes the ears of your heart will need the music of its poetry. And sometimes the thoughts of your mind will need the counsel of its greater wisdom. But whatever you bring to the Bible or require from it, the Bible always invites you to read below its surface as well, because the mystery of God is found not simply on the page, or within the text, but behind it.

In the churches of the Eastern Orthodox tradition there is a screen of icons called the *iconostasis* that separates the nave from the space containing the altar. In the *iconostasis* is a set of doors—the "royal doors"—opening to the sacred space behind, and above them there is always an icon of Christ enthroned in glory, *Christos pantokrator.* His image is placed above the doors specifically to invite the believer into the eucharistic banquet taking place not only behind the screen but also in heaven. On either side of the Christ, and sometimes gesturing in his direction, are flanking images: always the Blessed Virgin, and usually John the Baptist. They are there to indicate the way to the one who is the Way.

Consider this book to be like one of those supporting icons. It is meant to draw your attention to the mystery of the Word, but it is the Word itself that is the central invitation into the life of God.

Telling the Story

On Good Friday some years ago, one of my colleagues had a conversation with her five-year-old daughter about the events remembered in the liturgy of that day. With a sense of timeless immediacy that only children have, Sarah asked, "Mommy, were you at the crucifixion?" When Susan, Sarah's mother, said no, she hadn't been there, Sarah asked, "Then how do you know it's true?" Her mother explained that while she had not seen the crucifixion, others had, and they had told their friends about it, who told their friends, who told still others. On and on it went, said Susan, the story being passed along from friend to friend so that, down through the centuries, eventually she too was told the story. "Oh," said Sarah, "it's like a food chain." She was exactly right! It *is* like a food chain, a chain of never-ending storytelling that unceasingly feeds the community assembled to hear the Word spoken. It is the table around which the faithful gather to taste the presence of God.

That said, I am still intrigued by Sarah's need to have the crucifixion verified. However innocent her question, it reveals a skepticism—and not just on the part of children—that equates truth with eyewitness reporting and journalistic accuracy, and that is a thoroughly modern idea. Only in the last couple of centuries has the authority of the Bible come to be linked to its historical reliability. Only since the eighteenth century have we in the West come to link the reliability of history with the veracity of the historical reporter. And only recently have we come to evaluate the *truth* of an account in terms of its correspondence to events as they actually occurred. Withholding judgment until we have *checked the data* is a relatively new idea.

In antiquity, particularly the culture of the Near East from which our Bible comes, life was organized around sacred story and everybody knew that the stories contained details that did not necessarily correspond to fact. What the stories contained were *myths*—not in the modern sense of lies or falsehoods, but ordered truths that explain the universe. Myths were used to describe the beauty of the desert in bloom or the dark mystery of a cave. They could account for the periodic and predictable flooding of the Nile or the unpredictable waters that rip through the Judean desert in the rainy season. They could justify your good fortune or your bad. But primarily myths explained your relationship to the Divine.

Abraham, the first of the patriarchs of Israel, understood his life in terms of myth and would not have troubled himself with whether the story corresponded to what he saw in the world around him. For example, Abraham probably understood his God as the one who brought the world into being along the lines described in the creation myths of Genesis and who then re-created the world as told by the myth of Noah. He would not have read the stories, of course; they had not yet been written down. Abraham would have heard them in oral form, with the details undoubtedly shifting around in their telling and retelling. We do not know, of course, whether Abraham ever stopped to consider, as we moderns do, that six days for creation and forty days of rain are unlikely details—or if he even heard the stories with those particulars included. But if he did, I suspect he did not trouble himself much with the facts. The surface details of the mythic narrative were less important than the deeper meanings below them. Truth, after all, is never derived from bits and pieces of information but from the meaning we make of them. The whole cloth of truth is woven together from hundreds of threads of meaning.

Disregard for the facts in storytelling is hard for us to comprehend, yet we disregard them all the time. We all know family stories, for example, that through the generations have accumulated highly suspect details, but these embellishments do not in any way diminish the truth of the story. Quite the opposite: they tend to add depth and nuance to the truth of the myth carried by the story. None of us would dream of omitting the "good parts" just because their grip on the facts is a little weak.

When I was a small boy, I spent a part of each summer with my Uncle Lynn and Aunt Pat who had, as they used to say in midwestern farm country, "just gone to housekeeping" and were working one hundred and fifty acres in Clinton County, Missouri. I loved those visits, especially at milking time, and threw myself into the day's chores as though I were one of the hired hands. My efforts so impressed my Uncle Lynn that to this day, at every family gathering, he tells about my pulling weeds in the bean fields taller than I was. Over the years the story has been told so often and grown to such mythic proportions that as he tells it now, I was weeding fifty acres of soybeans singlehandedly, working from dawn to dusk, day in and day out, up and down the rows, one weed at a time, hands covered in blisters. Of course none of this is accurate—except the part about the blisters—and everybody knows it, including my uncle. But it is a story about the tenacity a ten-year-old can bring to a task that he is doing for an adult he loves, and so it is a true story despite the details.

We should think of the Bible as containing that kind of story. Most of the stories in the Hebrew and Christian scriptures are myths that contain deep reservoirs of truth beneath the surface. The four evangelists, for example, never intended to write historically accurate biographies; no chronicler in the ancient world did. Rather, they attempted to testify to a profoundly new connection to God that they had experienced in the person of Jesus. Each evangelist had his own particular experience, and each gospel has its own perspective, its distinct audience, and what we would call its unique theological agenda. Thus these stories do not necessarily provide a consistent picture of the man whose story they tell; often they conflict with one another. Some of those contradictions we can put down to the fact that different incidents in Jesus' life were differently remembered. Or, in some cases, one group of Jesus' followers placed greater significance on one memory than on another. But it appears as though the evangelists were also not above altering the details, and even inventing some, if doing so better communicated their deep belief in Jesus as Messiah.

Take, for example, the circumstances surrounding the messianic birth in Bethlehem.

> In those days a decree went out from Emperor Augustus that all the world should be registered. This was the first registration and was taken while Quirinius was governor of Syria. All went to their own towns to be registered. Joseph also went from the town of Nazareth in Galilee to Judea, to the city of David called

Bethlehem, because he was descended from the house and family of David. (Luke 2:1-4)

There are several problems with the "facts" here. First, there is no evidence in any existing contemporary record of a world-wide "registration," that is, a census, under Octavius Augustus. Second, Publius Sulpicius Quirinius—who may indeed have been in charge of a local census in Judea—was imperial legate for Syria from 6 to 7 C.E.,[1] but those dates do not fit with Luke's preface to the births of both Jesus and John the Baptist: "In the days of King Herod of Judea..." (1:5). By all accounts, Herod the Great died some ten years earlier, in 4 B.C.E. Finally, we *do* know from Roman taxation decrees and census records that people were "registered" where they were living and working, not in their ancestral hometowns. So, as the biblical scholar John Dominic Crossan puts it, "the journey to and from Nazareth for census and tax registration is a narrative fiction, a creation of Luke's own imagination, providing a way for getting Jesus' parents to Bethlehem for his birth."[2] But for the first hearers of these stories, that would not have been a problem. They would likely have disregarded the details and heard the more substantial truth beneath the story, which is Luke's conviction that this Jesus of Nazareth was the prophetic answer to the ancient Israelite hope for a future Davidic leader:

But you, O Bethlehem of Ephrathah,
    who are one of the little clans of Judah,

---

1. C.E. stands for "of the common era." I use this abbreviation, together with B.C.E. (before the common era) in preference to the familiar but more Christocentric designations for marking time, B.C. and A.D.

2. John Dominic Crossan, *Jesus: A Revolutionary Biography* (San Francisco: HarperSanFrancisco, 1993), 20.

> from you shall come forth for me
>   one who is to rule in Israel,
>   whose origin is from old,
>   from ancient of days. (Micah 5:2)

Matthew 2:6 explicitly quotes the Micah passage to explain why the Messiah was to be born in Bethlehem, and he does not locate the holy family in Nazareth until after their temporary stay in Egypt (2:23), thereby avoiding the difficulties raised in the Lucan text. But if Luke needed to create a "narrative fiction" to get Mary and Joseph to the village of David, I doubt that anyone would have quarreled with his imaginary construction.

Nor do Mark, Matthew, and Luke give any evidence of needing eyewitnesses to back up the truth of their stories. The author of John's gospel, on the other hand, tells us in the final chapters that he is concerned about what will happen to the story when there are none left who can tell it firsthand. The two big stories in chapter 20 of Mary Magdalene and doubting Thomas deal ostensibly with the issue of seeing the risen Jesus and believing that he is the Christ. But, more accurately, the problem addressed is believing without actually having seen. By now John is winding up his case for Jesus as Messiah and is concerned to promote its future. So it is not at all surprising that one of the final stories of the gospel brings a doubtful disciple to belief by inviting him to touch the wounds of the Risen One (John 20:24-29). That is an eyewitness experience *par excellence*. But it is even more to John's point, I think, that Jesus' last words in the chapter are those he speaks to Thomas: "Have you believed because you have seen me? Blessed are those who have not seen and yet have come to believe" (20:29). What follows is the evangelist's summation of his case:

> Now Jesus did many other signs in the presence of his
> disciples, which are not written in this book. But these
> are written so that you may come to believe that Jesus
> is the Messiah, the Son of God, and that through believ-
> ing you may have life in his name. (John 20:30)

Here John is alert to how difficult it might be for those of
us who have not, like Thomas, literally heard and seen and
touched the "word of life" (1 John 1:1). So he offers his
gospel to all those of a later generation who will not be able
to say "I saw"; the gospel becomes the *seeing* of Jesus the
Christ. In fact, John's closing words—"these are written so
that you may come to believe"—are an invitation to reread
the story, because by doing so we come to see Jesus more
and more deeply. We are also meant to pass the story on to
our friends so that they might know the story too, and
have life in the knowledge of its truth.

∼ Finding Our Way into the Story

When the fourth evangelist invites his readers into belief
through their encounter with the gospel, he places himself
within the timeless tradition of community-building by
way of storytelling. Believing communities are fundamentally communities assembled around sacred texts.
That word "assembled" connotes more, however, than a
simple gathering to hear the tales told, for these are the
stories that tell us who we are. They give us our identity.
We find in them the myths and deep mysteries that constitute the truest rendering of where we have come from,
how we ought to be, and where we are going. The stories of
the Bible are the past, present, and future for people in the
community of faith. That is what we mean when we use
phrases like "the authority of Scripture." The Bible is

authoritative because our experience tells us that its stories best explain who we are as a believing people and provide a record of our timeless relationship to God. Other stories fall short on both counts.

The distinction between our stories and the stories that fall short can be illustrated by an exercise that a colleague of mine once put to a confirmation class. In his instruction to the class, he made the point that the Great Thanksgiving of the Eucharist is a synopsis of our community story. Eucharistic Prayer A, for example, reaches back to the roots of our belonging *to* God, touches on our present separation *from* God, and looks forward to a redeemed future *with* God. It begins, he said, by alluding to Adam and Eve expelled from the garden, works its way down through the prophets to the present, and then imagines the second coming and the day of judgment. He then asked the members of the class to compose their own versions of the Great Thanksgiving, ones that would tell the other stories of our culture—the ones we find on television, in corporate boardrooms, on the diamonds of major-league baseball teams, on the advertising pages of our magazines, in the headlines of our daily newspapers, and on the Internet. Here is one of them:

> We give thanks to you, O God, for the goodness and love which you have made known to us in Hollywood; for money and power and popularity; for good looks, hard bodies, blond hair, and straight teeth; for the word spoken by *People* magazine; and for happy endings.

This is not a synopsis of the Christian story, but it is a story we recognize. It is not a story that assembles a sacred community, but it describes with insight our secular reality. And it is exactly this kind of story from which our sacred texts call us to turn away, or, to use biblical language, the kind of story of which we are asked to repent.

Another place where the sacred story assembles the community is in the liturgy of Holy Baptism. In the part of the rite known as the Examination of the Candidates (BCP 301-303) there is a set of six questions that presume the person about to be baptized has been properly in-structed—if an adult, directly; if a child, by proxy. Holy Baptism is many things, but minimally it is a rite of prom-ise giving, of covenant making, and the questions posed during the examination probe whether the candidates have been sufficiently prepared for the promises they are about to make.

In the ancient church, particularly in those first centu-ries before the emperor Constantine delivered the entire Roman world into Christian hands, the period of instruc-tion for baptism often lasted as long as three years. This prolonged period was required not so much by the amount of material to be taught, but by the community's need to be certain about the formation of an aspirant's character. Those first centuries were an era when Christians under-stood themselves as God's "kingdom-builders," standing in radical opposition to the dominant culture. Frequently they proclaimed that opposition stridently, so member-ship in the church was often considered seditious and com-munities were episodically persecuted. If you aspired to fellowship in one of the Christian assemblies you needed to know what you were getting into and the community needed to know what it was getting. Hence the long period of preparation and scrutiny, called the catechumenate.

Just as the early Christian community had a story to tell that was radically different from the stories of its wider world, so do we today, and the questions posed to the bap-tismal candidates in our modern liturgy retain the tone of that ancient community and its tensions with the outside world. The first three questions are called the Renunciations; they ask whether the candidates are prepared for repentance, for leaving the world's story behind and entering a new story shaped by the gospel. The second set is called the Adhesions; they ask whether the candidates understand what this new story is about. They are to imitate Christ's pattern of life: are the candidates prepared to live his story?

Following the examination, the community recites the Baptismal Covenant, which is the Apostles' Creed in question-and-answer form (BCP 304). I like to think it is placed at this point in the liturgy not so much as a set of doctrinal propositions to which the candidates are meant to give assent, but as a summary of the community story into which they are about to be welcomed. The more doctrinal of our two creeds, the Nicene Creed, contains weightier bits of theological reflection that took nearly five centuries to work out, while the Apostles' Creed derives from the simple affirmations spoken at ancient baptismal liturgies. It gives an outline of the history of salvation told by Holy Scripture: *creator of heaven and earth...born of a virgin...suffered under Pontius Pilate...crucified, died, buried, descended to the dead...rose on the third day...ascended into heaven...will come again.* No other story has quite this sequence of events, and it is altogether different from the stories the world tells us. In our own day, this story belongs as little to the world as it did when those earliest kingdom-builders told their version in opposition to empire.

This portion of the baptismal liturgy concludes with the Prayers for the Candidates (BCP 305-306), in which we pray that the catechumens will embrace the community story and live out its demands. Then, finally, into *this* story the candidates are baptized, as surely as the waters initiate them into the body of Christ. The story becomes their story, too. But even more is going on, because in the baptismal rite the stories of the newly baptized are added to the community story. In fact, each time there is a celebration of Holy Baptism, the church is made new again. Just as the community remembers its story as part of the celebration—reads the Word, hears it preached, recites the creed—that story is *re-membered*: the community is expanded and reassembled by a new story. The story of the newly baptized changes the community story—only slightly, perhaps, but changes it nonetheless.

∿ A Story of the Nation of Israel

Christianity is not the first religious community to have been "assembled" by its sacred texts; Judaism has prior rights to that claim. It too is a religion of the book and derives its identity from the telling and retelling of its story, beginning with the story of the Exodus. One of the most vivid descriptions of how a text brought together the Jewish community is given in the eighth chapter of Nehemiah, which recounts how Israel, after its return from Babylonian captivity, recovered its sacred identity.[3]

In the year 587 B.C.E. the Babylonian armies captured the kingdom of Judah, destroyed its capital, Jerusalem, with the Temple of David, and sent the defeated Judeans

---

3. Most of the biblical texts discussed in this book will require that you keep your Bible handy as you read. In fact, I urge you not only to read the text for which I provide commentary, but to read around it too; one icon helps illuminate another. But most important, mine is a secondary writing and no substitute for an encounter with the original material.

into exile in Babylon. The entire nation probably did not go into captivity, but certainly its leadership, comprised of the political, economic, and religious elite, did. When Cyrus of Persia came to power, however, he in turn defeated the Babylonians in 540 and permitted the Israelites to return to Judah and to their worship of Yahweh. Repatriation was effected in stages over more than a century. Ezra, a priest, came to Jerusalem late in the period of rebuilding with the endorsement of the Persian court to reestablish religious life in the face of considerable religious backsliding. With him he brought a copy of Torah, the law of Moses.

What we find recorded in Nehemiah 8 is a covenant-renewal ceremony over which Ezra presided. At the time of the autumn harvest festival, at a site of public gathering just inside the Water Gate of Jerusalem, the people of the city gathered to hear Ezra's version of Torah (Nehemiah 8:1-8). A platform was constructed for the ceremony and Ezra read from early morning until midday to what was, by all accounts, a raptly attentive audience. Alongside Ezra stood the Levites, prepared to give the "meaning" of the book in order that the people could "understand"—preachers, if you will, breaking open for the faithful the Word spoken by Ezra.

On the second day of Ezra's reading, the people began the celebration of the Feast of Tabernacles, *Sukkoth* in the Hebrew, which is also called the Feast of Booths because, as part of the festival, the people lived in temporary hut-like dwellings or tents as a reminder of their forebears' forty years of homeless wandering in the desert. This observance is commanded in Leviticus 23:42-43, but appears to have gone unobserved during the exile (Nehemiah 8:17). On subsequent days of the festival, while the people took up residence in the booths—as Orthodox Jews still do at *Sukkoth*—Ezra continued his reading. At the conclusion of the feast, the people confessed their sins collectively (Nehemiah 9:1-3), Ezra offered a lengthy prayer on their behalf (9:6-37), and a covenant document was signed by official representatives of the people (9:38).

It is not clear what Ezra read, but scholarly consensus suggests the Pentateuch, the first five books of the Hebrew scriptures. If that is so, Ezra can be regarded as "the architect of Judaism"; his contribution to the postexilic community was to establish the five books of Moses as authoritative for Jewish faith and practice. In short, he gave them their *canon*. "Canon" is a Sumerian word used of any measuring device—a carpenter's rule, for example. The Greeks referred to their classic literature as *kanones*, that is, "standards of excellence." Applied to the Hebrew and Christian scriptures, canon refers to literature that is both sacred and authoritative; it constitutes the community's history, faith, life, and conduct. The canon, therefore, is the collection of texts that assembles the community and against which all other communities and stories are measured.

In the end, it does not really matter which portion of the canon Ezra read; what matters is that reading some portion of it quite literally assembled the community or, more precisely, reassembled a community that had fallen into disarray. Its capital city and its temple were, of course, in shambles. But more important than the architectural clutter and chaos was the fact that during the exilic years Israel's corporate memory had lapsed. The fact that booths had not been built since the "days of Jeshua son of Nun" (Nehemiah 8:17) implies that the ancient community liturgies had fallen into disuse. Similarly, the people's confession of their own sins as well as "the iniquities of their ancestors" tells us that the laws of Moses had not been observed for some time. Thus the rapt attention with which the people listened to Ezra's reading makes considerable sense: these are people hearing their story told for the first time. I imagine Ezra standing before an astounded and speechless crowd, and by his reading, saying in so many words, "Listen to this. *This* is who we are!" And at the hearing of "the words of the law," as the book of Nehemiah records, the people wept (8:9)—as you weep when you have finally found that piece of yourself lost for so long.

～ The Exodus Story

Long before the time of Ezra, the nation of Israel was first brought together by the story of its escape from Egypt as told in the book of Exodus. This is its originating story, its myth of national origins. All of us know the outlines of this story, from the Nile turned to blood because of Pharaoh's hardness of heart to Moses' hand stretched out over the Red Sea to part the waters. I would argue, however, that the shaping character of the Exodus story, its power to assemble the people, extends well beyond those stories that run from the calling of Moses to the mired chariots of Pharaoh's armies. The Exodus was both a single historical event and a larger historical movement. As event, it was an action of God in history recorded first in Exodus 3-14 and then recapitulated in the songs of Moses and Miriam in chapter 15. This single action was, of course, the delivery of the Hebrew people from their bondage in Egypt. It was their founding experience, and the memory of that experience has served throughout the centuries to define Jewish identity.

As a larger historical movement, however, the Exodus was the ongoing experience of several generations that developed the identity and the historical memory of the people of God. This experience began with the flight out of

Egypt and continued through the wandering in the wilderness, the giving of the law at Sinai, the entry into Canaan, the conquest, and the apportionment of the promised land among a confederation known to us as the Twelve Tribes of Israel. The stories recording this larger movement take us quickly out of the book of Exodus, wend their way through the pages of Leviticus, Numbers, and Deuteronomy, and finally conclude with the last chapter of Joshua. Thus the myth of origins is not a single story but a collection of stories spanning perhaps hundreds of years. All the stories taken together—not one or two or three—form the identity of a new people called the Children of Israel.

Perhaps the most important episode in this entire saga is recounted in that last chapter of Joshua. In fact, this may be the most important chapter in all of the Hebrew Bible, because it is here that the narrative of the myth of national origins is finally completed. What happens in this chapter is not unlike the events described in Nehemiah; like Nehemiah, it is the record of a covenant-renewal ceremony. But it is also the record of the covenant enlarged. Joshua begins the ceremony by reciting the events of Israel's salvation history starting with the era before Abraham, when "your ancestors—Terah and his sons Abraham and Nahor—lived beyond the Euphrates and served other gods" (Joshua 24:2). He recounts the journey of Abraham and his family from Ur of the Chaldeans, around the arc of the Fertile Crescent, and down into Egypt. He summarizes the Exodus in roughly three verses, skips quickly through the wilderness sojourn, brings his hearers across the Jordan River at Jericho, and concludes with an inventory of the peoples conquered—in accordance with Yahweh's promise of land for Israel (24:3-13). This outline of history is not unlike Christians' recitation of the creed, which is also a summary of God's mighty acts on behalf of an elected people. Then Joshua challenges the people to decide whether they will serve Yahweh or the gods of the Canaanites: "Choose this day whom you will serve!" are his ringing words (24:15). There is unanimous assent in favor of Yahweh and a formal contract of obedience is drawn up: "So Joshua made a covenant with the people that day, and made statutes and ordinances for them at Shechem" (24:25).

It is an odd story. Does it imply that the children of Israel, so recently brought up out of Egypt, freshly delivered from their wanderings in the desert, and now victorious over the indigenous nations of Palestine, have such short memories? Have they so soon forgotten just who brought it all about? Perhaps. We are told that fidelity to Yahweh was not always a community hallmark during the long wilderness period. In the first blush of victory, with the ancient promise of a land now fulfilled, the people may very well have been tempted to abandon their covenant obligations to God in favor of the local Canaanite deities.

On the other hand, it might have been important that the originating covenant with Moses be renewed, now that the promise had at last been fulfilled. Joshua does not preside over a ceremony that brings Israel and Yahweh together for the first time. That relationship began at the mountain in the Sinai desert and ran its long road to Shechem; the making of the children of God out of this ragtag lot of nomads occupied the whole distance. So it was probably fitting that the end of the road be marked by a solemn renewal of allegiance. And that brings us to the part of this story which asks for an explanation: Why Shechem? Why that particular locale in the geography of this story?

Many scholars have observed that in all the stories about the conquest of the Transjordan and the Canaanite hill country there is never a mention of any military activity around Shechem (present-day Nablus, just north of Jerusalem). The Bible's silence on this point is intriguing, but particularly so in light of the report in Genesis that Jacob purchased a piece of land near Shechem and built an altar there to *El-Elohe-Israel*, "God, the God of Israel" (Genesis 33:20). *El* is also the name of the chief Canaanite god, and that coincidence suggests the presence of Hebrew tribes in Canaan long before Joshua who had entered into cordial relationships and maybe even common worship with the population of this Canaanite city-state (see Genesis 34).

Such an alliance between Hebrews and Canaanites would explain why Shechem need not have been conquered: it was already sympathetic to the invasion. If that is true, then the ceremony at Shechem recorded in Joshua not only *renewed* the Mosaic covenant but *extended* it to others not previously included. Hence the special force of Joshua's demand, "Choose this day whom you will serve!" He is speaking not so much to the children of Israel who had come up out of Egypt, but to those who had not, and that is the real point of the story. While the ceremony in Jerusalem recorded by Nehemiah reassembles the people of the covenant, Joshua's ceremony in Shechem enlarges the covenant by extending it to a new people. Then the important question becomes: how do you extend the covenant made by Yahweh to those who have not been children of the desert, who have not experienced the Exodus or tented along the lower slopes of Mount Sinai? By telling the story again, so that the story becomes *their* story, too. The Hebrews of Shechem are incorporated into the ancient story; the ancient story, told again, assembles a new community. The Mosaic covenant is not so much being remembered as the Exodus story is being *re-membered*. Retelling the story to new hearers is always meant to do precisely that.

I began this chapter with a story from Holy Week and I will end it with one from Eastertide. Years ago, at a midday eucharist on a Wednesday in Easter Week, I listened to the preacher retell all the resurrection stories in a single homily, weaving their threads of meaning into a single piece of cloth of mystery. I sat mesmerized, wrapped in the retelling of these familiar stories. It was a long sermon for a weekday service yet none of us really noticed the passing of time. We were *listening* to the stories. Later I asked myself, as I had done before, "What is the power of these stories?" These are the stories I have heard year in and year out, from my childhood. I have picked them apart in their original languages, preached them and prayed them, used them in teaching, in spiritual direction, and in pastoral care. Again and again I hear and tell these same stories, but I never tire of them. I am haunted by these stories, captured by them, held hostage to them, as though I were hearing for the first time: "On the first day of the week, while it was still dark, came Mary Magdalene early to the tomb" (John 20:1). Just the sound of those words never fails to strike deep chords within me.

What is the power of these words? It is actually fairly simple. These stories have a hold on me because they are *my* stories, just as they are *your* stories, and they are the stories of the family and the community to which we belong. They make sense out of our lives, our relationships, our world, and our God. They are our true stories.

Chapter 2

Passing on the Story

During the fiftieth anniversary year of the end of World War II, an advertisement ran in the *New York Times Magazine* for a collection of commemorative stamps issued by the State of Israel. The stamp featured in the ad reproduced a photograph taken on August 5, 1945 that depicted survivors of the Nazi concentration camp at Dachau just after their liberation by American troops. When I saw this picture of a crowd of people, still in prison uniforms, streaming through the barbed-wire gates, it struck me that this image was an icon of the Jewish community that had been formed by its sacred story. It is the story of a God who liberates them from oppression, slavery, and death.

The God who liberates is the God whose story is told in those texts of Exodus and Joshua and Nehemiah that we considered in the previous chapter. In fact, when Joshua asks at the Shechem ceremony that the gathered tribes choose which god they will serve, they emphatically decide for the God of liberation: "Then the people answered, 'Far be it from us that we should forsake the LORD to serve other gods; *for it is the LORD our God who brought us and our ances-*

tors up from the land of Egypt, out of the house of slavery'"
(Joshua 24:16-17, emphasis added). This is the historical
memory running beneath all the stories of the Hebrew Bible, the memory of a people who were oppressed and then
delivered. What historically set Israel apart from the other
nations was its experience of release, its coming out of captivity. Through that experience the children of Israel became a people whose identity was grounded in a God who
liberates.

So it was the Exodus story that came immediately to
my mind when I saw the Dachau stamp, but the advertisement itself was ambiguous. Over the picture of the freed
and bone-weary Jews ran, in twenty-point bold type, the
following phrase: "A stamp to help you remember what
should never be forgotten." "What, precisely," I asked myself, "should 'never be forgotten'? How many stories are
being told here?" I suspected there were two—not only the
Exodus story but the story of the Holocaust as well. Surely
the Holocaust, not the Exodus, was what the stamp-
collector should never forget. And that reminded me how
the story of any community is always being adjusted to fit
the community experience. The founding myths shift as
the lives of the people shift. In fact, the experiences that a
community goes through shape its people's stories, just as
the stories they hear and pass on shape them. Or, to phrase
it another way, the sacred community assembles its texts
as much as the sacred texts assemble the community. This
is by no means mere expediency, however, because the
community of faith is always in dialogue with its sacred
story, and experience is one party to the conversation.

The shifting role of a story in a community's life can
also evoke profound tension. I know of no better example
of that sort of tension than the political life of modern Israel, as I so vividly saw for the first time on a trip to the

Holy Land in 1994. We had arrived in Israel only a few days after political autonomy had been granted to the Palestinians in the Gaza Strip and Jericho, so the outcome of the fledgling peace was very much on everyone's mind. During this visit our group of mostly Christian clergy met with two leaders of the Knesset, the nation's parliament. One was a member of the conservative Likud party and the other was from the Meretz coalition, which occupies what we would call the left end of the political spectrum and had supported the Middle East peace process early on.

The Likud member took a very hard line in opposition to his government's peace initiatives at the time. No borders should be redrawn, no territories ceded, and no accommodations made. "*This*," he said, "will never happen to us again!" None of us needed him to elaborate: the *this* to which he referred was the extermination of six million Jews in the Nazi death camps. For him, the Holocaust was the story that had created the nation, and that is certainly one way of reading Israel's history. Had there been no Holocaust, the world community might not have otherwise endorsed the establishment of a sovereign state for the children of Israel. But this was not the conservative's only story; his insistence on holding onto what are called "the territories" echoed the biblical story of the promise of the land to Abraham and his descendants.

The Meretz leader took a different tack. She supported the initiatives for peace because of what it means to be a Jew. "A people brought up out of slavery," she said, "cannot enslave another people. We cannot hold the Palestinians hostage in what is their ancient land, too. The West Bank must be returned to them." For her, the formative story was the Exodus, and its memory must not be lost in an ongoing modern debate over how much land was really promised to Abraham exclusively for the Israelites or which territories Joshua actually occupied.

Another way to think about the dynamic between a people and its sacred story is to understand that the story is always being rethought, reflected upon anew, and reappropriated by each succeeding generation of the believing community. And reappropriation is by no means restricted to the political. An older rabbi friend who survived the Holocaust admits he is no longer able to think of the Yahweh of the Hebrew Bible in exactly the ways he was taught in his boyhood *yeshiva*. Because of the death camps, he has abandoned his earlier theology of an all-knowing, all-powerful God. A much respected teacher of Torah, my friend has re-membered—has taken his understanding of God apart and put it back together in a different way—a piece of the ancient story out of his personal history. I doubt that his is an isolated case.

Younger Jews, living in a different time and place, may reinterpret the story differently, or even appropriate altogether different pieces of it. For two of our three seminary years, a classmate and I took part in a monthly dialogue with students from Hebrew Union College in order to thrash out some of the differences between us and reclaim some of the common ground of our traditions. One session was given over to soteriology, or how God's saving power is revealed. This was a potentially prickly topic, because Christians cannot talk about salvation without talking about the cross. For us, the crucifixion is God's ultimate saving act.

Afterward a young rabbinical student came up to my classmate. "You have in the cross," he said, "the symbol of the God who chooses to suffer with us. We don't have that symbol in Judaism, and I envy you that. But isn't it possible that the cross could be the symbol for *all* human-

ity—the symbol that God is present *in* our suffering?"
That, of course, is a stunning piece of *Christian* theology.
The cross *is* the symbol of God suffering with us. While I do
not think that this young student was about to turn from
Judaism to Christianity, he was clearly rethinking his own
tradition in light of his people's centuries of affliction.

～ Rereading the Book of John

To rethink the sacred story is not, of course, a uniquely
Jewish occupation. Nor is it an exclusively modern one.
Communities of faith have been reinterpreting their stories over and over again from ancient times, and Christians
have been doing it since the beginning. This is everywhere
evident in our sacred scriptures, but perhaps nowhere
more dramatically than in the gospel of John. From one
perspective—though by no means the only one—John's
entire gospel is a work of reinterpretation. And, like the
stories of the Exodus and the Holocaust, it is a text
assembled out of a community in crisis.

It requires very little reading between the lines to see
that the Johannine community had a particularly complicated relationship with Judaism. Even the most casual
reader of John can see that its story is filled with tension
between Jesus and "the Jews" (better translated as "the
Judeans"), a term that is unique to this gospel. Sometimes
this tension is subtle, concealed beneath an otherwise neu-
tral narrative, as in John's version of Jesus' cleansing of
the Temple.[1] In the other three gospels, this story represents the climax of Jesus' difficulties with the Jewish and
Roman authorities and so it is placed at the end of his min-

---

1. Compare, for example, John 2:13-22 with Mark 11:15-17; the
   accounts are really quite similar.

istry. It is the fulcrum upon which the balance of events tips toward his suffering and death. It is Jesus' final insult, hurled at the religious and political establishment of his day, and the action that gets him arrested.

In John, however, the gospel more or less begins with a whip of cords whirled by an outraged Jesus at the merchants and money changers in the Temple (2:13-17). The episode is deliberately placed: by locating this incident early in the story, the author lets the reader know that the whole of Jesus' ministry will be surrounded by conflict. The cleansing of the Temple prefigures the passion to come. To use the literary term, the story is *proleptic*; that is, it *reads forward* to later events in the narrative. At the beginning of John's gospel, it is the authority of Jesus that scourges the Temple; at the end, the Temple authority will scourge Jesus.

In other parts of John's text the tensions with "the Jews" are far less subtle; hostility is right on the surface of the story. In John 10:26, for example, Jesus asserts that the Judeans "do not belong to my sheep." Or, in a far more acrimonious exchange, Jesus charges that the children of Israel are not heirs of Abraham or God the Father, but are children of the devil (8:44). Why such vitriolic language?

The community from which John's gospel came, like other first-century Christian groups, undoubtedly began its life as a small collection of devout, observant Jews. They had, of course, an altogether new and astounding experience of God through their experience of this odd man Jesus, but they still thought of themselves as Hebrews. They were, if you will, simply Jews who were *for* Jesus. So long as one remained faithful to Temple and Torah, there was plenty of room within first-century Judaism for pluralism—of political ideology, religious observance, and interpretation of the law. The New Testament writings hint at this diversity when they betray the competing theologies of, say, the Sadducees and the Pharisees. But after the year 70 C.E., when the Romans destroyed the City of David and its second Temple, pluralism became a problem. As is so often the case with religious communities under siege, the wagons of orthodoxy began to circle and a number of people were excluded, among them the Johannine Jewish Christians. Under the leadership of the Pharisees, Judaism now pinned its hope for survival on ideological conformity, and it was no longer permitted to be *for* Jesus and yet remain a Jew.

To this end, the rabbis altered the "eighteen benedictions," or what we might call "the prayers of the people." These prayers were read in the synagogues when Jewish men came to study Torah and to pray. The rabbis added to these a curse against the *minim* (that is, the "heretics") and the "Nazoreans." Thus members of the Johannine community found themselves beyond the pale, their names removed, as it were, from the Book of Life. Indeed, when it came his turn to read the new benedictions, the Johannine Jew had to make a choice: either decline to read, thereby placing himself *de facto* outside his community of origin, or pronounce the curse against himself and his new life in Jesus. Since they had never thought of themselves as anything but Jews, the Johannine followers of Jesus, now torn away from their religious roots, developed an understandable hostility toward "the Jews." This attitude finds its narrative expression in the belligerent animosity that the Jesus of John's gospel so often displays toward his fellow Jews. His words in these cases, however, are probably not authentic because they are clearly anachronistic; more likely they express the animosity of the Johannine community, whose words have been placed by John on the lips of Jesus, living about fifty years earlier.

The Johannine community, however, took another tack in coming to terms with its rejection by Judaism—and this is where the issue of revisioning commands our attention. Left without their Judaism, they were not left without their Jesus, and they began a systematic process of reinterpreting the former in terms of the latter. In fact, on one level, the singular purpose of the Fourth Gospel can be seen as a thorough revision of all Jewish tradition in terms of Jesus. No longer are the children of Israel fed with the manna of the wilderness; now Jesus is the bread of life (6:35). No longer is the law of Moses essential for access to God; "No one comes to the Father except through me," Jesus tells his disciples (14:6). John's gospel even redefines the Jewish festivals in terms of Jesus. At the Feast of Booths, for example—that festival which in the book of Nehemiah is so critical to the reassembling of post-exilic Judaism—Jesus goes up to Jerusalem and there says of himself, "Let anyone who is thirsty come to me, and let the one who believes in me drink" (7:37-38). This is almost certainly an allusion to Numbers 20:2-13, where Moses strikes a rock in the desert and brings forth water, which was read as part of the liturgies for the feast. But in John's rendering, Christ is the water of salvation, and his believers become channels of living water to others.

The events in the life of the John community were no doubt more complicated than I outline here. But whatever the exact circumstances, the gospel as we now have it is a record of a community that had reassembled its sacred texts, and it was absolutely essential to their life for them to do so. Although occasioned by crisis, their reappropriation of the Jewish story provided a way for the community to order a chaotic present, look with hope toward the future, and still retain its past—albeit a past that had been reimagined.

This crisis in the John community, however, played itself out in regrettable ways. Its hostility to "the Judeans,"
together with other and similar New Testament texts, became the scriptural underpinnings for Christian anti-
Semitism. As early as the second and third centuries,
Christian theologians began to speak of Judaism and pa-
ganism in more or less the same breath. No longer was the
Jewish community considered to be a participant in salvation history; no longer were Jewish interpretations of the
Old Testament credited; no longer was the Jewish background to the New Testament recognized. One second-
century ultra-orthodox sectarian, Marcion, argued that
the Christian church should abandon the Hebrew Bible altogether because of its revelation of a God of judgment—fickle, capricious, despotic, and cruel—and not a
God of love. Not surprisingly, attitudes like these served to
cripple the Jewish-Christian relationship for centuries.

Readers of the Bible need to remember that there are
some very unpleasant chapters in our sacred story. No
twentieth-century Christian of sensitive conscience would
agree with John's Jesus in claiming that the children of
Abraham are children of the devil. But it does us no good,
particularly in our relationships with our Jewish brothers
and sisters, to pretend that the author of John's gospel did
not put those words on the lips of Jesus.

I am often asked by readers of John's gospel just what
kind of meaning we should take away from our understanding of the conflict between ancient Judaism and the
Johannine community. Can we reinterpret these texts for
our own time and situation? In his book *Jews and Christians in Dialogue* John Koenig offers an eloquent option.
"Down through the centuries," he writes,

> Christians without number have found great strength
> in the majestic Christ of the Fourth Gospel. Large num-
> bers have come to faith through John's powerful im-
> ages. It would be profoundly wrong for us Christians
> to deny or denigrate the grace that has come to us via
> the pages of the book. Nevertheless, knowing what we
> do today about how... the Fourth Gospel unfolded, we
> must move (in the name of grace) toward working out
> a more adequate view of its authority in the church.
> Can we not accept the love of God through Jesus Christ
> without denying it to those who believe differently?[2]

What Koenig advises here is not so much that we reassemble the texts, certainly not literally, but that we reassemble
ourselves. That means we are to equip ourselves with eyes
to read and ears to hear the gospels so that we might discern in them what is primary and what is peripheral.
"With such sensitivity," Koenig writes, "we could, perhaps,
acknowledge both the blindness of the Gospel writer over
against his Jewish neighbors in the first century and the
Light of the world which shines through all darkness
(John 1:5)."

This is excellent advice in an increasingly pluralistic
world. Within a five-minute drive of where I used to live,
on a Friday evening I could see Hasidic Jews walking to
their synagogues and Muslims entering the Islamic Center
of Chicago. In a world where we are surrounded by believers whose sacred stories do not altogether overlap our
Christian one, we would do well not to bring our ancient
hostilities to bear on our present realities—especially since
the hostilities were themselves part of a particularly ago-

---

2. John Koenig, *Jews and Christians in Dialogue* (Philadelphia:
Westminster Press, 1979), 135-136.

nized historical moment and never central to the compassionate gospel of the Christ.

ᴖ Rereading the Book of Acts

Crisis, of course, does not have to be the only occasion for revisiting a sacred story. The Holy Spirit routinely prompts a *positive* rereading of the texts as well. A favorite of mine falls into this category: the story of Philip and the Ethiopian eunuch in the eighth chapter of the Book of Acts, a story that links word and baptism in precisely the way I discussed in the first chapter. The story is worth reading in full, so I suggest that you open your Bible to Acts 8 and read verses 26 through 40.

Luke, the author of Acts, is a great storyteller, and this has all the liveliness of his best stories. Every time I read it my imagination runs with delight over its visual images: Philip, newly ordained a deacon, is whisked from place to place by the angels and Spirit of God. An elegant courtier sits in his roomy coach and reads aloud, as in antiquity everyone did, muttering with confusion over the prophetic scroll. Philip, his interpreter, jogs alongside the chariot and answers questions on the run, until he is invited inside. Finally, the two of them go down into the water, out in a deserted place.

The story would have also captured the imagination of readers in the Hellenistic world. Luke addressed his two large works, both his gospel and the Acts of the Apostles, to this larger world, a culture fascinated by the exotic—geographical, ethnic, and sexual. Hellenistic culture was also highly invested in social rank and privilege. The Ethiopian eunuch thus satisfies as a literary figure on all counts. He was the keeper of his queen's purse, which made him a mighty person in his own land. His chariot must have been spacious enough for himself, a guest, and the scrolls, and he must have had a driver, too. How else could he have read while riding? His conversation with Philip, as it is recorded in *our* scrolls, suggests that he spoke rather elegant Greek. These details suggest that this story is a piece of early Christian apologetic literature—that is, an argument designed to build a case for Christianity against objections from its critics. It was no small part of early Christian propaganda to emphasize how its special claims met with approval from powerful people like the eunuch. He may have been exotic, but he was by no means despised in Hellenistic society.

What strikes me particularly about this text, however, is verse 35 and the action that follows it. Here is the verse: "Then Philip began to speak, and starting with this scripture, he proclaimed to him the good news about Jesus." The action that follows is this: "and both of them, Philip and the eunuch, went down into the water, and Philip baptized him." The eunuch, of course, is being baptized into the story of the Good News of Jesus. The story of Jesus is now *his* story. The text is assembling a new community, even if in this particular instance it is a community of only two. Notice also that the baptism is preceded by a period of catechesis, of teaching—albeit considerably shorter in comparison to the three-year catechumenate that came in the later centuries of the church.

But there is something else going on in this narrative that is equally marvelous. Even if the educated gentile world did not despise the eunuch, Judaism of the first century did—as in all likelihood the earliest Christian Jews did as well. In the Jewish world, the eunuch was at the very edges of social acceptability. He was, first of all, from "among the nations"; if not technically a gentile, he belonged to the "scattered ones" of God (Zephaniah 3:9-10).

Regardless of how often he might have made his pilgrimage to the Temple to worship, he would have had to stand in the Court of the Gentiles. And, even if he had been a Jew, his sexual mutilation alone would have kept him outside the shrine, as it was decreed in Deuteronomy 23:1. The eunuch's interest in the sacred books might classify him as a "God-fearer," someone who took the worship of Yahweh seriously, but that was not sufficient to erase his "uncleanness." The story, as Philip would have known it from his Jewish youth, was absolutely clear on this point: the grace extended by Yahweh operated exclusively within the sphere of the circumcised. God did not dwell among the nations. The eunuch may have occupied a central position of power in the court of the queen, but he occupied a position of powerlessness at the edge of the nation of Israel. And there Yahweh does for him what God has always done: he empowers the powerless.

So on the one hand, Luke's story is simply the timeless Israelite story of the God who liberates. The sacred story remains intact. On the other hand, the story is now also slightly rewritten. What it now says, reading between the lines, is that circumcision is peripheral and the liberating power of God is primary. The text has been *reassembled*.

This story dramatically represents a wondrously complicated dynamic between the community of faith and its sacred story. We come to the story from the distant and desert places of our lives as the Ethiopian came to Philip, hungry and thirsty for the Word. In hearing the story, in telling it to others and guiding them into a deeper understanding of it, we come to know who we are. We tell the story over and over because that is what it means, in the words of the baptismal covenant, to follow in the apostles' teachings. That is what it means to pass on the tradition.

But we are always rereading the story, too, in order to find out what is primary and what is peripheral. We are always transforming the text so that the text will transform us. When that kind of transformation occurs, reflectively and prayerfully, it is not a tampering with the text but the movement of the Holy Spirit. The movement of the Spirit enlivens the community and keeps the sacred texts "reading" us. Passing on the tradition, being faithful to the apostles' teachings, is less like conservation than like parenting. Good parents, it is said, provide their children both roots *and* wings. Holy Scripture is not an ossified treasure handed down from one generation of curators to the next; its treasure lies in what we make of it and what it makes of us. The sacred story has always invited an interpretive conversation between itself and the people it shapes, so that a new story can reassemble a new community for a richer life in God.

Chapter 3

Making the Story Our Own

When the General Convention of the Episcopal Church, newly independent of the Church of England, met in September of 1801, it adopted a slightly modified form of the Thirty-Nine Articles of Religion. These are the founding documents of Anglicanism and emerged from a late-sixteenth-century attempt by the Church of England, newly separated from the See of Rome, to express itself as both catholic and reformed. Article VI states, in its Elizabethan prose, "Holy Scripture containeth all things necessary to salvation: so that whatsoever is not read therein, nor may be proved thereby, is not required of any man" (BCP 868). In other words, Scripture, and Scripture alone (*sola scriptura* was Luther's phrase), is authoritative for faith. If you can't find it in the Bible, you don't need it for salvation. The wording of Article VI was largely shaped by the attitudes of the Protestant reformers, both in England and on the Continent, who felt that Roman Catholicism had corrupted the historical faith by burdening the believer with a number of "extra-biblical" doctrines, such as papal supremacy and purgatory.

Anglican scriptural theology is not as reactionary now as it was in the first blush of the Reformation, but it still speaks of Scripture as "authoritative." I would like to think that what we mean by the term today is that Scripture is authoritative because it says something transforming, both to individuals and communities. When we are touched in our very being by a passage or verse of Scripture, or even a single word, we have made it our own and, more important, we ourselves have been remade by virtue of the encounter. The passage is then *ours* in a way it has never been before, and we are no longer the same. That experience of Holy Scripture is authoritative.

Making the story our own is not an altogether easy thing to do and it will not happen every time we open our Bible, hear its stories read, or listen to its messages preached. In fact, many of us find the Bible more intimidating than any other book that sits on our library shelves. And more often than not the Bible does just that: it sits there. We all have one, but we hardly ever open it. Perhaps we find its contents impenetrable—accessible, we think, only to the professional scholar with years of training, including a mastery of Hebrew and Greek, if not also Coptic and Aramaic. By and large, we let these professionals read the Bible for us and, as a result, the Word has already been interpreted by the time we meet it.

I do not mean to diminish the importance of biblical scholarship; it is essential to our reading. Much of the Bible *is* impenetrable without a certain set of reading skills. But the problem with relying only on professional help is that it can work to insulate us from our own transforming encounter with Scripture. Professional Bible scholars cannot create for us an enlivened, Spirit-filled rendezvous with the Word merely through their own interpretive reporting, however well-informed and erudite that reporting might be. In fact, I think that seminary professors, parish clergy, and preachers should think of themselves not as dispensers of information about what is *in* the Bible, but as facilitators who assist others in their attempts to embrace the Word that moves *out* of the Bible to touch the life of the reader.

Bible readers in Christian communities do not so much need *experts* as they need *adepts*, skilled readers who can both instruct and inspire us with their own passion for the Bible. The difference between the two was illustrated in a lecture I heard once by the church historian Richard Norris, who used an example from music. When Itzhak Perlman gives a master class on the Mendelssohn E-minor Concerto for Violin and Orchestra, he can impart considerable esoteric knowledge about the piece, passing on ideas about interpretation, use of dynamic range, and particular strategies for the complicated bowing demanded by the intricacies of the score. As such, Norris told us, Perlman teaches as an *expert*. On the other hand, he may choose to help his students appropriate his skill so that theirs become greater and their involvement with the score will move from managing the techniques of performance to genuine passion for the music. He can help them bring their own voices to the song. In that case, Perlman is an *adept*, not merely an expert, and his teaching is motivated by a desire to make other adepts. ("Would that all God's children could play the Mendelssohn E-minor Concerto!" says Norris.) Similarly, the biblical adept is a skilled reader who can not only pass on technical information about interpreting the text but also nurture the transforming desire and delight that God and the readers of the Word are meant to have for one another.

Bible reading is also a community activity. Like the Mendelssohn concerto, the Bible is a piece written for full orchestra, not just solo violin. The book itself, after all, is the community's book, and we should read it together. Only when we approach the text collectively and share our responses to it are we each able to hear the deep resonances that sacred story sounds in the lives of other believers. This experience both corrects and expands our individual response to the Word. It corrects because community reading keeps our individual reading from becoming idiosyncratic; it expands because the more we read the Bible together, the more its meanings are opened up to us.

Another reason why making the text our own is so difficult is that we do not really listen to it carefully, precisely because we think we already know what it says. This is ironic. On the one hand we claim to find the Bible difficult and opaque, and on the other we think we know its stories well because we have been hearing them for so long. But often what we hear is itself derived from inaccurate *listening*. What most of us have as our Bible knowledge is a set of rough outlines of the stories, with many of the details mixed up.

The technical word for this mixing of details is *conflation*, and the most vivid illustration is probably the Christmas crèche. Think of the one you bring out every year, each piece lovingly unwrapped after its long hibernation in tissue paper. There is the Holy Family, of course, and the angels, the shepherds, the wise men, the animals, and perhaps also—if yours is like mine—a little banner with the words *Gloria in excelsis Deo* that you can hang over the top of the stable.

Now, if you sit down and carefully read the stories of Jesus' birth in the second chapters of both Matthew and Luke, you may be startled to see that the shepherds and the sheep, the angels and the *Gloria* are found only in Luke's version; they are absent from Matthew. Similarly, only Matthew's version has the astrologers from the East; there are no wise men in Luke. Even the stable and its crib are the property of only one gospel: the Jesus of Matthew is born in a house! The tradition of the crèche has "conflated" the narratives, mingling the details of the two stories together. That is what we frequently do with our own readings of Scripture: we construct a "nativity scene" of narratives. I frequently find myself in study groups where someone will make a point about the meaning of a text, and someone else will counter, quite emphatically, "But we know that Jesus says...." And I have to intervene with, "Not in Mark, he doesn't. He says that in Luke, but not in *this* text."

But perhaps what gives us the greatest trouble in appropriating the Word is that we stand at such a great distance from it, both chronologically and culturally. Anyone who has traveled in the Middle East begins to get a small measure of this distance. Not so much in cities like Jerusalem, much less Tel Aviv, but if you have been to a Bedouin encampment in the Negev or a Maronite village in Lebanon, where the liturgy is still celebrated in Aramaic, you begin to feel as alien in those settings as its people would feel in ours. And that's *now*, not then!

Modern readers tend also to overlook the fact that Jesus stood at as great a distance from much of his sacred story as we stand from ours. On September 25, 1995, when the Jews began Rosh Hashanah, their new year's observance, they also inaugurated a celebration of the "Year of David," the three-thousandth anniversary of the founding of Jerusalem. That historical benchmark, whether precise in its chronology or not, reminds us that the cultural distance between the Israel of the patriarchs—a millennium or more *before* David—and the Israel of Jesus' day must have been very large indeed. Abraham and his people were nomadic herdsmen and shepherds, loosely associated in tribal confederations for mutual economic dependence and episodic military defense. So too, most probably, were those Israelites who came to unite under the monarchy of David. First-century Galilee, by contrast, was a highly structured agrarian society shaped by Greek culture and ordered by Roman colonial and Jewish religious law. In fact, recent archaeological finds reveal that the Galilee of Jesus' time was by no means the rural peasant backwater that the religious folklore of our Sunday schools has portrayed. Rather, Galilee was a richly cosmopolitan center, and if Jesus indeed grew up in Nazareth, he was an easy four-mile walk from the recently excavated Roman city of Zippori, which boasted a theater, a gymnasium, a set of public baths, a large urban marketplace, and a number of wealthy private homes decorated with some of the most beautiful mosaics to be found in Israel.

All of this underscores that the Jews of Jesus' day were likely to have had as much difficulty with owning and interpreting their biblical texts as we have today with ours. Scholars currently analyzing the Dead Sea Scrolls report that those documents reveal as much variety of interpretation and debate as you would hear at any professional meeting of religious scholars and Bible critics today. The question of how to read the Bible is by no means a modern dilemma.

So, even before we begin to read, we discover that the voice of the Spirit carried by the Word is muted by the scholarly filters of professional readers, by inattention to what the words really say, and by cultural distance. There are other difficulties, of course, but if we could conquer these three we would be well on our way to appropriating our sacred stories.

The way to conquer these difficulties lies in a field of study that scholars call *hermeneutics*, or the art of interpretation. It is a venerable word, with its lexical origins in the Greek of classical antiquity and its etymological roots in mythology. It derives from the name of Hermes, the messenger god. Fundamentally, the term refers to the particular attitudes and ideas one brings to the reading of a text; it is the intellectual framework out of which one reads. If, for example, you use the skills of the literary critic when you read and seek for meaning in a text, you have a literary critical hermeneutic. If your primary concern is finding in the Bible a way of proclaiming the Good News that it conveys, you have a hermeneutic of evangelism. If you are a theologian of liberation, your reading is likely to be shaped by a hermeneutic of liberation. Now there is even a term for those who question all interpretations and are skeptical about finding intrinsic meaning in any text: it is called the "hermeneutic of suspicion."

In any case, hermeneutics denotes the specific points of view—the biases, if you like—that the reader brings to reading. *Bias* is not a bad choice, actually, because whatever the interpretative framework for reading, the reader needs to keep in mind that Hermes was not only the reliable messenger but also the god of highwaymen and thieves. A "single hermeneutic" reading will tend to mask the rich complexity of the text; it levels the contours, making the rough places smooth and the crooked ways straight, to paraphrase a biblical theme. If the adepts in your reading community tend over time to offer only a single interpretive point of view, be suspicious—they are making off with your text!

～ The Three Senses of Scripture

What I wish to do in the remainder of this chapter is offer some strategies that can help you to read and interpret

Scripture in order to make it your own. The process begins with reading the Bible for what I call its three senses: the literal, the historical, and the prophetic, or spiritual. This three-part reading strategy looks for the literal, historical, and prophetic meanings of a given text. I would like to claim the approach for my own, but I learned it first from Pablo Richard, a Chilean theologian who was one of my teachers. Since then, I have been developing the strategy and using it in my own teaching. It is, I think, a good tool for overcoming the initial barriers to Bible reading.

The Literal Sense
Any piece of writing, the Bible included, once delivered out of the hands of its author, has an independent life that stands free of any attempt to understand or explain it. It is its own creature, with weight and character, depth and nuance. Actually, this can be said of any product of creative activity. Ask a painter, for example, to interpret one of his canvases and he will tell you that the painting has a life of its own beyond explanation. To understand this about a picture or the chapter of a book or any piece of art is to appreciate its *literal sense.* This is the text as text, speaking its own voice. I also like to think about reading the Bible with this understanding as reading the *present* of the text. What I mean by that is attempting to encounter the now of a passage as you find it lying fresh on the page, without attachment to any past hearing of it and free of any expectation about what you might hear if you read it again tomorrow.

A check on whether you are reading for the literal sense is always to ask yourself a few simple questions. What does this passage *really* say? Am I conflating the details, or mixing it up with some other passage? Am I bringing some particular point of view or bias to my reading? A negative example may help clarify the point. So pause here, pick up your Bible, and have a look at Luke 16:1-9.

This passage tells the story of an estate manager who is accused in the first verse of squandering the owner's goods. The owner terminates his employment and demands a final accounting. The manager, in turn, approaches each of the owner's debtors and reduces the amount they owe, "so that, when I am dismissed as manager, people may welcome me into their homes" (16:4). Christians are often troubled by the manager's "dishonest" behavior in this story, and this affects the way they interpret it. The truth, however, is that the text never actually says he is "cooking the books." The story renders no negative judgment and there is nothing to suggest that the manager was stealing from the owner on his way out the door.

While most translations refer to the steward as "dishonest" in verse 8, and in verse 9 Jesus recommends that we make friends with "dishonest wealth" to gain eternal reward, the Greek word in both cases is *adikos*, which can also be rendered as "unrighteous," "unreliable," and "untrustworthy"—none of which explicitly adds up to financial malfeasance. In fact, the manager is commended for his fiscal shrewdness. Perhaps what he was really doing was reducing the debt owed the owner by an amount equal to some portion of his own commission as collector, thereby ingratiating himself with the debtors. In any case, this story is most commonly known as the parable of the unjust (or dishonest) steward, a title that betrays inattention to the literal reading sense. Thus, the title interprets the story even before we read it, which robs the text of its independent voice. Reading for the literal sense is by no means a *literalist* reading; it simply recognizes and honors what the text has to say for itself, unencumbered by anything we might bring to it.

The Historical Sense

There are at least two aspects of the historical sense of any biblical text. The first is the history *of* it, and the second is the history *behind* it. While I believe the second is ultimately more important for textual appropriation, it is helpful to know something about the first as well. In either case, to read the Bible for its historical sense is to read the Bible as *past*.

Most of our sacred texts have a rich history. Many, particularly the stories of Jesus' ministry, no doubt circulated in oral form within the early communities of believers and were written down only years after his death and resurrection. The written versions in turn were edited and then edited again—*redacted* is the technical term. The analysis of the editorial history of a text is called redaction criticism, which has been something of a cottage industry among Bible scholars in this century. This kind of criticism, for example, has shown that John's gospel went through a number of versions—at least four—before we got it in its present form.

One of the reasons that this kind of information can be helpful is that it assists in our understanding of what is primary and what is peripheral in any given passage. Some passages in the Bible, for example, have been deliberately altered in the redaction process by copyists of later centuries—scribes of perhaps small imagination who would alter a word or a phrase if the passage seemed to them difficult or obscure or out of synch with their own theological ideas or social sensibilities. An example of this sort of tinkering may be Paul's now notorious passage in 1 Corinthians 14:33b-36, where he forbids women to speak in church. In some of the ancient manuscripts, however, these verses are located in a different place—after verse 40. Since these words are also inconsistent with Paul's understanding of the equality of men and women stated elsewhere (for example, in 1 Corinthians 7:2-4), they are of doubtful authenticity. They were probably added to the letter by a later generation less sympathetic to the leadership of women in the Christian community.

In addition to having an editorial history, every text is situated within a specific historical context; this is the history that stands *behind* the text. Every passage of the Bible comes out of a specific time and place with its own sociology, anthropology, theology, economics, and politics. Another way to think about reading a text for these historical fingerprints is to read "contextually." An understanding of the means of production in ancient Near Eastern city-states, for example, helps shed light on the meaning of slavery in Egypt and on the Exodus experience of the Hebrews. Similarly, one should keep in mind that the gospel narratives come out of a century marked by profound political turbulence and social upheaval, especially in Galilee.

Understanding these dynamics is particularly useful in reading the New Testament passages known as apocalyptic texts. While this material deals ostensibly with the *eschaton*—the "end time," that great and terrible day of the Lord when God will bring all things to a cataclysmic conclusion—the apocalyptic genre was also a very popular vehicle for interpreting current events during the Hellenistic period. Frequently the historical review was inserted into the account of the apocalypse itself.

That is what seems to be going on, for example, in Mark 13:1-8, 14-23, commonly referred to as the "Little Apocalypse." I suggest you pause here and read all of Mark 13, focusing particularly on the verses noted above.

Here Jesus' disciples ask him to describe for them the signs of the end. In response, Jesus predicts the destruction of the Temple in Jerusalem and warns that there will be wars and rumors of wars, political upheavals, and natural calamities. He cautions his followers against false messiahs, warns that discipleship will occasion persecution, but consoles the faithful with the assurance that in the end the elect of the Son of Man will be gathered by the angels.

The historical background for this material is almost surely the Jewish-Roman War of 66–73 C.E. Palestine had been the site of episodic popular rebellion throughout most of the first century. Frustrated by more than a hundred years of Roman oppression, the peasantry was ripe for war. So when a revolt broke out in Jerusalem in the year 66, it spread quickly to the nearby provinces. In November of that year, Cestus Gallus, the Roman legate of Syria, marched on Jerusalem and occupied the northern edge of the city but was unable to take the Temple Mount at its center. Stunned, he retreated and suffered severe losses as Jewish guerrillas pursued him to the Mediterranean. Euphoria followed: Palestine was liberated, the rebels had turned away the colonial oppressors! The liberation proved to be short-lived, however, and the Roman general Vespasian was subsequently dispatched to "pacify" Palestine.

Vespasian marched six thousand troops south from Syria and north from Egypt. Although scattered guerrilla forces offered fierce resistance, much of the countryside, including Galilee, was reclaimed for Rome, and by June of 68 the armies were poised to take Jerusalem. Once again, however, the unexpected occurred: the attack was abandoned. Nero had been assassinated, four candidates vied for succession, and Vespasian was summoned back to Rome, having been proclaimed emperor by his legions in

Caesarea. Jewish resistance would get another reprieve of nearly a year and a half. In the meantime, there was reason to believe that Yahweh had intervened yet again, working not one but two miracles to save the Holy City.

During this grace period, there were probably rebel supporters moving around Palestine and calling the faithful to battle, portraying the war as a sure sign of the advent of the messianic age. It is also possible to imagine that the community from which Mark was writing would have wrestled with the question of where it should place its allegiances when these "wars and rumors of wars" were tilting the political seesaw back and forth. Could they be sure that the inevitable renewal of Roman action would be the "final fight"? Thus, the writer of the gospel places this urgent question on the lips of the disciples: "Tell us, when will this be, and what will be the sign when all these things are about to be accomplished?" (13:4).

Josephus Flavius, a first-century Jewish historian, records that there were a number of leaders of the rebel coalition who had competing ideologies, each vying for adherents—among them John of Ghiscala, Judas the Galilean, and Simon bar Giora. Some of their rhetoric included messianic claims, perhaps prompting Jesus' warning in this passage against false prophets and false messiahs who will lead "if possible, even the elect" astray. Here, against the background of apocalyptic metaphors, Mark is counter-recruiting, challenging the grounds upon which Jews are being conscripted into a putative "last battle." He even admonishes his community to abandon the idea of defending Jerusalem altogether, which is what I think is intended when Jesus advises his disciples that "those in Judea must flee to the mountains" (13:14).

Luke's gospel contains a parallel warning that is more explicit:

> When you see Jerusalem surrounded by armies, then
> know that its desolation has come near. Then those in
> Judea must flee to the mountains, and those inside the
> city must leave it, and those out in the country must
> not enter it. (Luke 21:20-22)

I suspect that Luke's narrative offers more specific detail because by the time his gospel was written, some ten years or so after Mark's, Jerusalem had indeed been surrounded by armies. The "desolating" sacrilege that Jesus only predicts in Mark had by the time of Luke become a reality. Thus, when Jesus offers an apocalyptic warning concerning the destruction of the Temple in Luke (21:6), his prophecy is *ex eventu*, after the fact. Luke's text here is yet another example, like those discussed in chapter one, of the evangelists "inventing the details" of their Jesus stories.

In either case, you can see how reading a passage while paying attention to its historical context can help open up and elucidate a text. In fact, I think that the more one reads for the historical sense of the Bible, the more one sees that the people of its pages were trying to struggle with the ways and will of God in their ordinary and extraordinary lives, which is our struggle too. And that brings us to the last of the three senses of Scripture.

The Prophetic Sense
To read the Bible for its prophetic sense is to use the text as an instrument for discerning God's presence in our lives now. A prophetic or spiritual reading asks such questions as: Where is the God of this passage or story today? Where is God leading us? What is it that God delights in for us? These questions ask the words of the text to be an expression of the Word in *our* world.

We read the Bible for its spiritual sense in order to appropriate anew foundational stories for the shaping of our
present lives and communities. If you think about it, that
is what is going on in the "Little Apocalypse" of Mark, although there was a different set of stories for Mark's community to consider. For them, a messianic age probably
meant a sovereign Israel, with the Romans expelled and the
Davidic monarchy restored. Mark rejects those stories as
idolatrous. Long before we get to chapter 13 in his gospel,
we know that Mark has already developed a different and
paradoxical story about power as ultimate powerlessness
and about life coming out of death.

> He called the crowd with his disciples, and said to them,
> "If any want to become my followers, let them deny
> themselves and take up their cross and follow me. For
> those who want to save their life will lose it, and those
> who lose their life for my sake, and for the sake of the
> gospel, will save it. For what will it profit them to gain
> the whole world and forfeit their life?" (Mark 8:34-37)

Mark's messiah will not sit on David's throne but reign
from Calvary. And so when Jesus directs his disciples to re-
ject the temptation of salvaging Jerusalem, Mark is commanding faithfulness to his alternate vision and
demanding of his community a prophetic reading of the
"texts" of their own lives. He asks the erstwhile followers
of Jesus to ponder the question "Where is God in all of
this?" His implied answer is, "Certainly not with a John of
Ghiscala or a Judas the Galilean!"

When we read the Bible for its prophetic meaning, the
passages we read become, in the very best sense, *canonical*.
They become a way to measure and assess the where and
how of God in present reality. If Bible reading is cut off
from its spiritual sense, however, by insisting that it has no

significance for our lives today, the texts become remote and our experience of God abstract. Ultimately, the point of the prophetic reading is to allow the texts to transform us, to reshape our lives, to turn us from idolatry to faithfulness. You can read the Bible for information alone, although that is probably not a legitimate approach to what is fundamentally a religious document. But to read without attention to the possibility of *conversion* is an indefensible posture for the community of faith. Thus, to read the Bible for its prophetic sense is to read for our *future* as children of God and heirs of the kingdom.

Reading the Bible for its spiritual sense is what gives life *to* the text and correspondingly allows the readers to find their own lives *in* the text. The prophetic, however, must always work together with the literal and the historical readings. In fact, reading for the literal alone tips toward fundamentalism, risking a future drawn upon an inadequate understanding of the past; fundamentalism is essentially ahistorical. But reading for the historical alone leaves us with little more than biblical archaeology; we end up knowing a good deal about ancient Israel but not very much about God. Reading for the spiritual alone tends toward the idiosyncratic and private; it looks to a future cut off from both the past and the present and can lead to strange and intensely personal interpretations. To appropriate the Bible fully, the believing community needs to read it for all three of its senses. Think of the three senses of the Bible as forming a triangle and imagine that you can place your reading inside it. Kick around a little; touch all three sides. You will begin to experience God past, present, and future.

Chapter 4

Breaking Open the Word

What I have introduced so far may sound simple enough, but at this point it is still a *strategy* for Bible reading, an approach but not yet a *method*. In this chapter, therefore, what I want to do is examine how the strategy can work in reading the Bible and then develop a method for applying it. We will begin with a pair of texts, which we will probe for the three senses I introduced in the last chapter: the literal, the historical, and the prophetic. The two texts I have chosen are both from the gospel of Mark: the first is the story of the Gerasene demoniac (5:1-20) and the second recounts a debate between Jesus and the Sadducees about marriage (12:18-27). We will also see what it is like to apply two different hermeneutics to these texts—two different kinds of "lenses" through which we will look at each passage. The first story we will read from the point of view of liberation theology, that is, from the perspective that the God of this narrative is the God of the Exodus, who liberates from oppression. We will read the second story from a feminist perspective, that is with an ear for listening to the voice of the divine feminine speaking from within the text.

Other points of view are possible, of course, but I have found that for me these allow for the deepest probing of these particular passages. I have been reading and teaching—to a wide and diverse spectrum of students—a political approach to the gospel of Mark for about a decade and find that it affords the only coherent interpretation of the entire text. Other hermeneutics work here and there, but reading through the political lens, be it feminist or liberationist, provides consistent meaning in Mark. In fact, I think Mark is "reading Jesus" through the lens of contemporary, grassroots politics and with an ethic for his community that is radically egalitarian. You do not have to be convinced by that argument, but I trust you will find it intriguing.

～ The Gerasene Demoniac: No One Could Bind Him Anymore

Exorcism is one of Jesus' healing ministries that figures prominently in the gospels. He is forever being called upon to cast out demons, including seven from Mary Magdalene, one from an epileptic boy, and another from the daughter of a Canaanite woman. Episodes like these have inspired an extensive scholarly literature on the subject of Jesus the exorcist, but scholarship is not necessary to make the point. On their own, the biblical reports attest to the power of Jesus over the spirits of darkness. His power over demons is so profound that it is they, not Jesus' followers, who are able to recognize him as "the Holy One of God." But what is the precise nature of this power? The exorcism of the Gerasene demoniac, I think, begins to answer that question.

This story also contains more detail than any other incident recorded in Mark's gospel except for the passion narrative at the end. That fact alone suggests that the healing of the demoniac was an extremely important piece of tradition held in the memory of Mark's community, and so it may offer considerable insight into how Mark understood Jesus.

But first, the story. Open your Bible to the fifth chapter of Mark and read verses 1 through 20. You may also want to compare the text with its parallels in Matthew 8:28–9:1 and Luke 8:26-39.

Reading for the Literal Sense
The first thing to pay attention to in this story is its geography. It is important to be alert to this because Mark makes very sophisticated use of what I call "the narrative geography" of his stories. The specifics of place often carried significant meaning for his original audience—most of which is lost on modern readers, either because most of us have not actually seen the terrain or its original associations are no longer current. Jesus has come to a place called the "Decapolis," specifically, to the "country of the Gerasenes." The Decapolis was a region mostly east of the Jordan River that was comprised of ten primarily gentile towns; the word *decapolis* means "ten cities." One of these was the town of Gerasa. Additionally, Mark makes other telltale allusions to a gentile setting. The phrase "the other side" in the very first verse, for example, alerts us to the fact that Mark is moving Jesus outside the symbolic space of Judaism. The inclusion of pigs—as opposed to "clean" animals like sheep or goats—and the fact that the demoniac is living in a graveyard both point to the uncleanness of gentiles. The gospels of Matthew and Luke tell roughly the same version of this story, although Matthew has a *pair* of demoniacs and locates the events in the town of Gadara, which sits on a bluff above the southeastern shore of the

Sea of Galilee. All three gospels thus agree on a narrative that takes place outside Galilean Judaism, thereby expanding the sphere of Jesus' ministry.

Perhaps the most striking bit of detail Mark gives us is that the demon has a name: *Legion*. "My name is Legion; for we are many" (5:9). Luke chooses to clarify Mark's account by adding "for many demons had entered him" (Luke 8:30). But clarification is not really needed, for legion is a Latin word with only a single meaning in the social world of the gospels: a legion of Roman soldiers. Alerted by this clue, we begin to discover other military references. For example, Jesus releases the legion with a military command: he "dismisses" them into the swine. They, in turn, rush over a cliff and fall into the sea.

It is hard not to hear echoes of the Exodus story in that sentence; Pharaoh's armies also charge pell-mell into a body of water that becomes their grave. That image is underscored in the Greek text with its word for "herd," *agele*, which can also be translated as "a band of recruits." Actually, *herd* is a curious choice; pigs do not travel in herds. But its oddness reminds me of a rule of thumb for reading: when you encounter a verse, a phrase, or even a single word that is troubling, when the syntax is awkward or the grammar is tortured, pay attention! Something important is probably going on. Bible scholars have a term for this: *lectio difficile*, the "difficult reading." Generally, the difficult reading is to be preferred because it usually means that the author is telling us something marvelous is hidden between the lines. In the case of Mark's choice of *agele*, I suspect that the second meaning of the word is encoded in the first: for those who have ears to hear, a band of Roman recruits is a demonic force.

Reading for the Historical Sense

I indicated in the previous chapter how significant the Jewish-Roman War of 66-73 C.E. must have been for Mark's community. In fact, that war was the culmination of a series of popular uprisings and peasant revolts that began with the death of Herod the Great in 4 B.C.E. and erupted episodically throughout much of the first century. In classic colonial fashion, Rome maintained exclusive and irksome authority over domestic affairs—including, for the peasantry, an especially beleaguering system of tributes and taxes—by way of its alliance with local client kings such as Herod, and its ever-present garrisons. The collusion of Jewish leadership with Roman power was probably nowhere more infuriatingly evident than in the billeting of Roman troops adjacent to the temple in Jerusalem, poised to crush any signs of insurrection.

This collaboration between the military occupiers of Palestine and the Jewish ruling class is, I think, central to the social and political background of Mark's gospel. His account, for example, of the beheading of John the Baptist (6:17-29) at the hands of Herod Antipas, one of the sons of Herod the Great, is itself both an indictment of the contempt that the Jewish nobility had for a Jewish dissenter and a caricature of a brutally capricious elite. In the case of the Gerasene demoniac story, I think that the narrative of the exorcism is Mark's specific but subtle literary attack on Roman colonial militarism.

We know from Josephus that a Roman garrison was stationed at Gerasa to defend the trade routes that ran along the eastern shore of the Jordan and to keep the encroaching Parthian empire at bay. Its numbers were considerably augmented during the time of the Jewish rebellion, so it is not at all surprising to find in this story cryptic allusions to Roman soldiers as demonic forces. Furthermore, Josephus records that during the revolt of the late 60s, Galilean guerrillas drowned a number of Herodian nobles—descendants of the dynastic house of Herod the Great—in the Sea of Galilee. In taking revenge on the Galilean rebels, the Roman general Vespasian dispatched several regiments to Gerasa who killed a thousand men, took their families captive, and plundered much of the local property. If we understand the exorcism as a symbolic assault on just that kind of Roman military violence, we are not at all surprised that Mark's herdsmen want Jesus out of their territory (5:17). They know the scorched-earth policies of Roman retribution.

When you look at this passage with an eye to its sociological dimensions, other implications emerge as well. In agrarian societies like Mark's, where a small, aristocratic elite commandeers the lion's share of what the vast peasant class produces, the symptoms of economic exploitation are frequently dismissed by the economically entitled as "demonic possession." Alternatively, scholars who read for the sociology behind Mark's story argue that possessed behavior can be a socially acceptable form of protest against, or escape from, oppression. Here is one socioeconomic analysis of the Gerasene demoniac:

> The tension between his hatred for his oppressors and the necessity to repress his hatred in order to avoid dire recrimination drove him mad. He retreated to an inner world where he could symbolically resist Roman domination. Jesus' disruption of the prevailing accommodation brought the man's and the neighborhood's hatred of the Romans out into the open, where the result could be disaster for the community.[1]

In other words, it is the danger of the hatred exposed by Jesus that prompts the frightened locals in the story to demand his departure. This idea is especially intriguing when you realize that Mark's story actually says very little about the demoniac's cure. Instead, it focuses on the disease, elaborately characterized as self-inflicted bruising and howling among the tombs. Perhaps the phrase "for he had often been restrained with shackles and chains, but...no one had the strength to subdue him" (5:4) is especially significant: the man breaks free of the fetters of oppression by his escape into madness.

Ched Myers, in his book *Binding the Strong Man*, suggests that the Gerasa miracle is the second of two exorcisms that Mark uses to inaugurate, in symbolic narrative form, his particular political agenda for Jesus. The first is the healing of the man with an unclean spirit in the synagogue at Capernaum (1:21-28). That story also locates Jesus in an alien and hostile place: he invades the sanctity of the domain of the Jewish scribes. The tension of that healing narrative, symbolized by the possessed man, is between the authority of Jesus' teaching and that of the scribes. Given Mark's narrative bias, the tension is naturally resolved in favor of Jesus: the man is relieved of his demonic spirit.

In Mark's hands, then, these two exorcisms can be viewed as a form of attack on the social world outside his gospel—against Roman military occupation in the Gerasa story and against the religious elitism of Second Temple Judaism in the exorcism at the synagogue. Mark's gospel is rather like a richly nuanced cryptogram, encoding in its story world the details of Mark's social world. And Mark's Jesus, in turn, wipes the Palestinian landscape clean of its dominant politics and its prevailing piety in order to estab-

---

1. Paul W. Hollenbach, "Jesus, Demoniacs, and Public Authorities: A Socio-Historical Study," *JAAR* 49:4 (1981), 573ff.

lish an alternate social reality—what he will call, as the gospel moves forward from these stories, the "kingdom of God."

Reading for the Prophetic Sense
If we accept these literal and historical readings of the story of the Gerasene demoniac, it is not too difficult to read its prophetic sense. Building the kingdom of God involves "wiping the landscape clean" of economic exploitation and class oppression, political domination and colonial occupation. A powerful example of reading the story in this way was told to me by a friend who spent a good deal of time in Nicaragua during the 1980s at a time when the Sandinistas were besieged by counter-revolutionary *Contra* guerrillas. On one visit, he was part of a Bible study that met in a poor barrio of the capital, Managua. One night his group read aloud Mark's story of the demoniac.

A member of the group was an illiterate *compasina*, a peasant woman whose husband and four sons were among the many Nicaraguan peasants killed during the conflict and termed, in the officialese of government reporting, "the disappeared." Right after the verse in which Jesus names the demon ("My name is Legion; for we are many") the reader paused. As he did, the woman echoed back his reading with, "My name is *Contra*, because there are so many of us." The story of the demoniac was now the widow's story too. In that moment she had listened to the Word becoming flesh, and in her hearing of it, Managua and Galilee became one in time and place.

It is not necessary, of course, to be living in a Central American slum in the midst of a bloody civil war to appropriate the Gerasene demoniac as one's own story. First-world Christians can just as easily ask *Legion* to name itself. Where is the demoniac of economic exploitation in the neighborhoods of our urban poor? Where do we collude with the demons of oppression in our political process? Where is the shackling of the mind in our schools and of the spirit in our churches? And where are our "swine-herds" who anxiously oppose the unmasking of the powers of darkness? Mark's story draws sharp attention to our dependence on, indeed, our addiction to, habits of economic entitlement and personal power. These are stalwart twentieth-century Western demons, but we dare not name the truth of them for fear of wreaking havoc on all that is comfortably familiar in our social world. The devil you know is easier to live with than the God you might meet.

There is one final piece of the demoniac story that has profound prophetic implications. The healed man, who wants to stay with Jesus, is sent away to proclaim the good news of his healing, to tell his friends "how much the Lord has done for you" (5:19). This directive bears a recurring gospel fingerprint: it encapsulates how we are to respond to the healing miracles of Jesus. We come to him, or he to us, from the very margins of our lives, from our ragged edges of brokenness, from our demonic places of oppression, and we are made whole by his presence. Once relieved of our demons, however, we are not meant to fall on our knees in adoration and hold onto him. Rather, we are meant to exercise our new power; healed, we are available for service. That is what discipleship is all about.

〜 Tying It All Together

You can still visit Gerasa today. It is Jerash in modern Jordan, located about eighty kilometers north of Amman and perhaps the best preserved and most extensively restored provincial Roman city anywhere. I made that visit with three friends and cannot leave the Gerasene madman behind without recounting how I think the site bears on the narrative.

Jerash is stunning. It has better survived the seismic activity of the centuries than other ancient cities of the region, so much of the sense of its original civic glory remains. We took turns speaking from a marble slab, center stage, at one of its two theaters; on that same spot an orator of antiquity would have stood. The theater is still acoustically perfect. Along the main street we passed the massive Temple of Zeus and another dedicated to Dionysus, over which the Cathedral of Theodora was built later, in the Byzantine period. Eventually we came to the Tetrapylon, a massive four-cornered marker at a crossroads. It indicates the four directions an ancient traveler could have taken into the rest of that vast Roman world: north to Damascus, south to Philadelphia (now Amman), east to Baghdad, and west to Jerusalem.

I have been in no other ruined city that so dramatically reveals the wealth and power of Rome in the provinces it occupied. Mark may very well have wanted to challenge that dominance by locating his most extensive exorcism narrative in Jerash. There is one problem, however: there is no major body of water anywhere nearby in which to drown the pigs! For that, you have to go to Gadara, as Matthew does. Ancient Gadara, or, in modern Arabic, Umm Qais, was also one of the cities of the Decapolis. It was never as populated or as prosperous as Gerasa, and it did not blossom fully until long after the time of Jesus, in the second and third centuries. It does have close at hand the sea required by our story, however. The mountaintop ruins of Gadara overlook the point on the modern map where the borders of Israel, Jordan, and Syria meet. Due north, and immediately across the valley below, is the southern end of the Golan Heights, and only slightly to the northwest is the Sea of Galilee.

What are we to make of these two locations—Gerasa at the center of Roman wealth but removed from the water, Gadara on the edge of the sea but hardly a symbol of provincial power? Here is what I suspect may have happened. Early on there was a story widely circulated in the oral tradition about the healing of a possessed man that took place somewhere in the region of the ten gentile cites. The transfer of the demons to the swine may also have been a part of the original story; then, as now, the problem with exorcism is where to put the evil spirits once you have cast them out! The pigs may have been included to add color to the story or to provide ironic symmetry: the unclean into the unclean. In any case, the memory of an incident and the outline of a story came first, before the gospels; the evangelists gave definition and detail later. That statement is, of course, a small piece of redaction criticism; it attempts to offer something of a history for the texts as we have them now.

For Mark, the political geography of the story was crucial. He knew perfectly well that Gerasa was nowhere near the Sea of Galilee, and his hearers knew that too. But his choice of Gerasa for the drowning of the demons was easily justified on symbolic grounds: he needed a center of Roman power as the scene of his narrative attack. Matthew, however, did not share anything like Mark's passion for the political. In any case, by the time Matthew wrote his versions of the Jesus stories, the political urgencies had passed: the Temple had been destroyed and Jerusalem lay in ruins. So Matthew may have abandoned political invective in favor of topological verisimilitude and thus the demoniacs got moved to Gadara.

A caveat or two, however. First, there are a number of ancient manuscript versions of Matthew's text that agree with Mark in locating the story at Gerasa. Gadara may be a later scribal "correction." Editors by nature have a tendency to even out stories that authors leave ragged. Second, archaeologists argue for a number of sites for the demoniac story up and down the eastern Galilean shores. Third, I need to admit my own biases in both the thrust of my reading and my interpretation of the geography: my understanding of this text is shaped by the hermeneutic of liberation. I do not apologize for that; I just name it as such.

Finally, you may notice in this "summing up" section—particularly in bringing my visits to Jerash and Gadara to bear on the texts—that I have blended together at least two of our reading strategies, the literal and the historical, and added a third: geographic inspection of the story sites. If you will, I have been kicking around inside the reading triangle, touching all of its sides, trying to get a sense of its contents, and determining its size. And that is precisely how interpretation is done.

∾ "Like Angels in Heaven": Against Levirate Marriage

The second text I offer is very different from the first, although it is also from Mark. It is not a miracle story but, ostensibly, a theological debate between Jesus and a circle of his critics concerning the resurrection of the dead. The story is found in the twelfth chapter of Mark, verses 18 through 27. Take a moment to read it now.

The idea of resurrection came late to Jewish thinking and was not everywhere embraced. From early in Israel's religious history, immortality was understood to reside in posterity, which is one of the reasons why ancient Judaism placed such a high premium on family and children, especially male children. The Pentateuch makes no reference to resurrection at all. Acts 23:8 says that the Pharisees held to a doctrine of the resurrection but the Sadducees did not. In short, the Bible is rather sketchy in its presentation of theological material pertinent to resurrection—except, of course, for the unambiguous declaration in the New Testament that Jesus was raised from the dead. All of which makes Mark's text a potentially significant contribution to the topic. Or is it?

Reading for the Literal Sense
This is not an easy text to decipher. Even attending carefully to its details, you come away thinking you understand only half of what is going on. It is obvious that there is some conflict in the passage; biblical scholars refer to this text as a "controversy narrative," and it is one of many used by the evangelists to establish the authority of Jesus over the religious leadership of his day. In fact, when you read the stories that come before and after this one, you discover that the Sadducees are preceded by the Pharisees, who approach Jesus on the volatile topic of Roman taxation (12:13-17), and succeeded by the scribes, who question him about the Great Commandment (12:28-34). After the third interchange, "No one dared to ask him any questions" (12:34b). Authority established!

The exchange between Jesus and the Sadducees is in the ancient style of formal rabbinic debate. According to its rules, one party poses a question with reference to some point of the law, and the other rejoins not by answering, but by posing a different question supported by a different scriptural citation. This is where the modern reader can run into trouble, because Mark not only assumes a depth of scriptural knowledge that most of us do not have, but he also credits his reader with knowing something about how the rabbis used their texts. So, some assistance with the biblical allusions and the rabbinic arguments from scholars and commentaries is in order.

The teaching of Moses to which the Sadducees loosely refer is Deuteronomy 25:5-10, which outlines the rules for so-called levirate marriage (from the Hebrew word for brother, *levir*). When a family in ancient Israel acquired a wife for the eldest son, the primary motivation was to secure an heir. If the son died without issue and had surviving brothers, it was the duty of the next eldest brother to marry the widow. The first son of the levirate union, however, was considered to be the child of the deceased, not of the brother who biologically fathered him.

It is against the background of these legal strictures that the Sadducees rejected resurrection. In fact, they thought the whole idea absurd because it created the potential for moral chaos in the afterlife, and in Mark's passage they offer the example of the woman widowed seven times as a case in point. God's law surely would not allow for such confusion. From our perspective, however, their reasoning looks specious. In fact, when you extend the case to seven brothers dead, each one of them childless, the Sadducees seem to be reducing the argument to absurdity.

In responding, Jesus ignores their argument and quotes not from Deuteronomy but from Exodus 3:6: "I am the God of your father, the God of Abraham, the God of Isaac, and the God of Jacob." The thrust of this rejoinder hangs on the tense of the verb *to be*. If God *is*, not *was*, the God of Abraham, Isaac, and Jacob, there must be resurrection, since, says Jesus, "He is God not of the dead, but of the living" (12:27). If the patriarchs are alive with God, then so shall everyone be. The thread of this argument is virtually identical to the one followed by the rabbis contemporary with Jesus who *did* conclude from their readings of Torah that there is resurrection. That congruence works in Mark's hands to establish Jesus as a credible teacher—at least within some rabbinic circles. But note that the Exodus text does not actually say that the patriarchs are alive, only God is. So even Jesus' argument is a little twisted.

That aside, what is all the fuss about? Why is it important for Jesus to provide an argument for the legitimacy of resurrection based on Torah? Is Mark ensuring that once we get to his story of the empty tomb, we will not find it inconsistent with rabbinic reasoning? Surely not. And would that argument not be a little cryptic in any case? Most people are not likely to embrace a resurrection faith based on the tense of a single Hebrew verb. The first witnesses to the Risen Christ certainly based their convictions on experience, not syntax! So the controversy in Mark about levirate marriage appears to be a trifle specious, even a sham. When Mark lets us know in the very first verse that it is the Sadducees who "say there is no resurrection," it is hard to credit anything they say. The reader knows that the Sadducees' minds are made up before the discussion begins, and—like the Pharisees before them—they simply want to entrap Jesus "in what he said" (12:13). So what *is* going on?

I think this story is about two things. The first is a teaching about transformation in this world, not the next, and the second is about relationships on earth, not in heaven. I rely on a pair of narrative clues for my interpretation. One clue has to do with word choice. At the beginning of the exchange, Mark has the Sadducees speak of *resurrection (anastasis* in the Greek), a noun that carries the sense of a static theological abstraction. But when Jesus speaks of "the dead being raised" (12:26)—*egeirontai* in the Greek—he literally means "the being-raised ones." Actually, you do not need the Greek to see the distinction. Attention to the literal sense of the text reveals even in translation that the noun "resurrection" is associated with the Sadducees and the verb "to be raised" is used by Jesus. The verb is active—it suggests not an intellectual proposition but a transforming action. I do not believe for a minute that this shift is an accident, certainly not with a writer as skilled as Mark.

The second clue is provided by the phrase "they neither marry nor are given in marriage, but are like angels in heaven" (12:25). One of the more embarrassing readings of this text in the history of Christian interpretation, based on the juxtaposition of angels and marriage, concluded that human sexuality disappears in the afterlife. The Sadducean dilemma therefore becomes moot, because the resurrection life is without gender distinctions, sexuality, or sexual intercourse. In this state of being, the ethical problem of simultaneous multiple marriages disappears.

I do not think that this is what the passage is saying at all. Rather, I suspect that to be "like angels in heaven" is to live in God's world. Or, more precisely, to live in a world transformed more by what God has in mind for humanity than by what humanity has in mind for itself. That does not mean a world without sexuality, but a world without the concept of sexual property. And that is why Jesus speaks here about marriage and also about being *given* in marriage. The distinction between the two will perhaps become more obvious if we turn to the historical reading of this text.

Reading for the Historical Sense
Perhaps the most important piece of history behind this text is the social role of the Sadducees in first-century Ju-

daism. They were, as our literal reading has already suggested, a theologically conservative sect that considered only the Pentateuch to be authoritative and binding. They eschewed the rest of the Hebrew Bible: the historical writings and the prophetic books. Since the Five Books of Moses have no specific words on the matter of resurrection, it is not surprising that Mark would have the Sadducees pick a fight with Jesus about it.

The Sadducees were also the rich, landowning patricians among the Jews of Roman Palestine, although their influence may have been in decline by the time Mark's gospel was written. They were the elders of the community, the clerical and lay nobility. The chief priests of the Temple came from Saducean ranks and the Talmud says that "they held all the treasure, their sons were the treasurers, their sons-in-law were the managers, and their slaves beat the people." A bit more oblique in his judgment, Josephus writes that the "Sadducees have the confidence of the wealthy alone, but no following among the populace." There would have been no love lost between the Sadducees and someone like Jesus, a man from the artisan classes of Galilee.

Levirate marriage worked in favor of the interests of the aristocracy; it served to continue the patriarchal family and to compound and concentrate its landed wealth. Mark, as we have seen, is no defender of the established social order, so it is no wonder that the only time he brings the aristocratic Sadducees onto the stage is in an argument that has less to do with questions about the next life as with maintaining the status quo in this one. Mark's passage is indeed a controversy narrative, but the controversy is not about doctrine.

Reading for the Prophetic Sense
What is at issue in this text is the desire to ensure one's socio-economic status, and the levirate law worked admirably in this regard. One can argue that this patriarchal institution was motivated by concern for the economic interests of the widow, but is it not patriarchy itself, by which the woman has no identity apart from her father and husband, that gave rise to the need for protecting the widow in the first place? In a different social order, where the woman is not *given* in marriage—where she is person, not property—ideally her interests would be assured by virtue of her equal social and economic status. New Testament scholar Elizabeth Schüssler-Fiorenza explains that Jesus' notion of a heaven without marriage does not mean "that sexual differentiation and sexuality do not exist in the 'world' of God, but that 'patriarchal marriage is no more.'"[2] The god of patriarchy is a god of the dead, while the God of Israel—the one Moses met in the burning bush—is a God of the living. In a world rich with God's life women will no longer be treated as nameless objects, and the Sadducees' question as to whom the woman belongs—"In the resurrection, whose wife will she be?" (12:23)—has no meaning.

When we read Mark's text prophetically, it calls us to read the texts of our own lives with a similar hermeneutic, which we could also call a hermeneutic of mutuality. But when we read our own texts, we find that the god of the dead has not everywhere given way to the God of the living in our culture. Sexism, sexual harassment, and sexual violence are continuing realities in our world. Although many churches recognize this reality through social outreach,

---

2. Elizabeth Schüssler-Fiorenza, *In Memory of Her* (New York: Crossroad, 1985), 144.

such as supporting shelters for battered women and their children, the feminist hermeneutic bids us question why such shelters are needed at all. Is not the need to protect the abused wife, so often regarded as the sexual property of her husband, only a modern version of the need that occasioned levirate marriage in ancient Israel? Is not the fact that there are battered women at all a consequence of a culture that continues to value men more highly than women? Such questions require us to examine our public and private rhetoric of equal access and equal opportunity and see it for the thin veneer it often is. Deeply rooted in our myth of national identity is the conviction of the shared dignity of all humanity—a biblical concept. But more often than not, as individuals and as a nation, like the Sadducees, we abandon companionability in favor of casuistry.

∼ The African Bible Study: A Method for Community Reading

Once a strategy for reading the Bible through various interpretive lenses is in place, how do we use it? Strategy by itself is not enough—a method is needed so that the strategy can work in the reading life of the sacred community. There are several good methods available for Bible study in the parish setting, but here I will focus on a modified form of what is called the African Method. This method reads Scripture on three levels: the words of the passage, its historical context, and its meaning for us today. These three levels of reading are meant to capture the literal, historical, and prophetic senses outlined in the strategy above. Together, the three ways of reading help us to appropriate the present, the past, and the future of the text in the life of our reading community.

This method also assumes that those in the study group will be *hearers*, not merely readers, of the Word, and that literacy per se is not required for the Word to speak. To begin our study of the Bible by simply *listening* to the text, before anything else, directs our attention to the literal sense of the passage. Listening also places the reader in the position of the audience for whom these texts were originally written: they were hearers of the stories, not readers of them. Even when a written text was available, such as one of Paul's letters, it would have been read aloud to the assembled community.

Here is the method. With the members of the group seated in a circle, a text from Scripture is read aloud three times. After the first reading, each person in turn is asked to speak a word, a phrase, or a whole sentence that conveys an idea, feeling, or image from the reading that particularly captured his or her attention. Nothing else at this point is required, and commentary by others on someone's word, phrase, sentence, idea, feeling, or image is not allowed. What you are listening for in this first round of reading is what the text *says*; you are listening for the literal, and it is stunning in how many wonderfully various ways the reading will be heard.

The passage is then read again. After this second reading, the floor is open for free discussion and reflection on its content and meaning; this is also the point at which the discussion leader can reserve the right to direct conversation by being didactic and instructive. This part of the method—*exegesis* of the text—will occupy most of your study time. *Exegesis* is the term Bible scholars use when they mean "interpretation," probing and penetrating the text to reveal its depths. Exegesis is a sacred task. John's gospel calls Jesus the interpreter of God: "No one has ever seen God. It is God the only Son, who is close to the Father's heart, who has made him known" (1:18). In the Greek, *exegesato* is the verb; so, literally, the Son "exegetes" the Father.

This portion of the study, after the second reading, is the time to struggle with the meaning of words, to compare translations, to wrestle with difficult turns of phrase. It is the time to talk about the text in terms of what you bring to it from previous readings, how you have heard it preached, what the church—including your third-grade Sunday school teacher—has said about it, and what you do not like about what the church has taught about it. It is also the time to bring to the text what you know and can learn about ancient history, Greek poetry, first-century Palestinian politics, Roman law, the medical anthropology of illness in the ancient world, the role of women in the early church, agrarian land reforms in third-world countries, and the editorial in yesterday's newspaper. Bring all these to your reading; the text can bear the weight so long as you are attentive to what it really says. Unlike the ancients, we are not an aural people, so this is also the point where I would relax the rule about listening only and open your Bibles—*but not until you have listened to the passage twice*.

Once the group has thoroughly explored the literal and historical meanings of the passage—or, more likely, once the clock shows the session will soon be over—read the text for the third time. Each member of the group is then asked either to offer some particular prayer that has emerged from the readings or to reveal some way that the passage has prompted the beginnings of some kind of personal transformation.

That may sound difficult, since many people are timid at first about speaking their inmost thoughts, but praying out of the Bible is not really as daunting as it first seems.

Often it is nothing more than restating what you said after the first reading, although now you may have a richer response than at the beginning. When the Nicaraguan widow named the Legion as *Contra*, for example, she was praying out of her anguished connection to the crucifixion. Almost anything that connects the circumstances of your immediate life to the text is its own kind of prayer, so do not hesitate to speak it. That, according to St. Paul, is the Holy Spirit praying within you. I remember a Bible study in which a woman in the group simply said, "I am glad to have found something new in this old story." That was a prayer of praise.

Finally, someone in your study group should gather the prayer concerns and reflections into a closing *collect*, a "collecting" prayer. This prayer is important because just as one does not read the Bible alone, in the end one does not pray it alone. Reading the Bible in the sacred community is ultimately an act of community worship, so community reading should lead to community prayer. The Holy Spirit moves through the whole reading community, not merely the individual reader.

Chapter 5

Forming Community Character

A parishioner once told me that he had read the entire New Testament in one sitting for the single purpose of finding the so-called good news in it. "I didn't find it," he said. "Nothing but a collection of indictments! You are constantly being condemned for where you stand and called to stand in some new place." His assessment is largely accurate. Repentance and conversion *are* major themes of the New Testament, and if we go to the Bible to find out who we ought to be, not just who we are and who we have been, then it follows—if we read prophetically—that its texts will call us to move from the present to the future, and the two are not likely to be the same.

The community of faith has always looked to Scripture for guidance in shaping its ethics, and for good reason: the Bible has considerable ethical content. The most common problem in using the Bible as a resource for ethics, however, is that we often come to its pages not for advice on who we ought to be but for endorsement of who we are. Often we hunt for a scriptural passage—usually taken out of context—that seems to support an ethical position we have already taken. In fact, we tend to make up our social values as we go along, deciding which are meaningful and which are not, and then we impose them on the pages of the Bible. Our feet are firmly planted on what we have decided is high moral ground, and we ask the Bible to defend our turf.

The specific term for this is "prooftexting," that is, finding a text that proves the point. The more general and technical term is "eisegesis," which means reading *into* the text rather than reading *out* of it. If exegesis is the process of finding out what the text says, eisegesis is the process of finding in the text what we want it to say. Eisegesis can be done with any text; it is the slippery slope of all Bible reading, but I think we do it more frequently with texts that seem to be about morals than with any others. When it comes to use of the Bible for ethical debates, we more frequently allow our cultural values—whatever they may be—to interpret God rather than allowing God to inform our values.

If we are to avoid this misstep on the road from who are to who we ought to be, the first thing Bible readers need to appreciate is that the word *community* is key to any discussion of biblical ethics. That is because the Bible, on the whole, is more concerned about community character than individual moral quandary. Religious ethics in our churches, by contrast, has come to focus more on the terms of individual salvation, making faith a private matter separate from public life. In our culture, we are preoccupied with individual options and tend to ignore the larger area of corporate choice. And when we focus on personal moral dilemmas, Jesus becomes "the answer" only to our private questions. Admittedly, the later New Testament material—especially the epistles of Peter and

James—betrays concern for individual moral posture. But by and large, the gospels are less interested in where the individual will stand in the future than in where the church stands in the present. If the Bible is at all a primer on ethics, it is a users' guide for how to shape the life of the community. Thus, in this chapter I want to explore some scriptural passages that I think highlight the Bible's concern for community character.

～ Personal Quandary and Community Character

The gospel writers first care passionately about whether the discipleship community is egalitarian in social arrangements, resists injustice and oppression, and is radically inclusive. These concerns emerge in a difficult passage found in both Matthew and Mark that has, I believe, often been misinterpreted. Open your Bible and read the parallel accounts in Matthew 18:6-9 and Mark 9:38-49. Actually, read Mark first, then Matthew, because this passage is a good example of how Matthew takes up and then varies a text that probably first belonged to Mark.

The *HarperCollins Study Bible* labels the part of this passage about stumbling blocks "Temptations to Sin." That is not an altogether inaccurate way to interpret the narrative, but sin in this instance has a highly specific meaning that requires some attention to the historical sense of the text. Recall that the Markan community, where this story originated, found itself caught up in the fiercely competing ideologies of a highly politicized Galilee on the eve of the Jewish-Roman War. As a result, the community faced at least two urgent issues: first, what should the nature of its relationships with outsiders be? and second, what should its stance be on insiders who defect? These are the questions that Jesus addresses here.

First, on the literal level, what is happening in this passage? The exorcist whom the disciples tried to stop has been using Jesus' name to endorse his own brand of charismatic healing, and Jesus' disciple John thinks that the disciples have exclusive claim to that charism. The amusing irony in John's attempt to draw a boundary around the community of compassion is that the disciples—just ten verses back (Mark 9:28)—tried their own hands at exorcism without success. More to the point, though, Jesus has just reproved them for bickering about status and prestige (9:33ff). But John still does not understand: he wants to lead, not follow, and he is troubled by potentially powerful competitors. This is an astounding misapprehension, given that Jesus has just clarified for him the character of the kingdom community: "Whoever wants to be first must be last of all and servant of all" (9:35). Jesus, rather than consenting to John's designs for excluding the "unauthorized" exorcist, draws the community boundaries more widely: "Whoever is not against us is for us" (9:40). He welcomes all who work mercy and justice; the borders of the kingdom must be permeable.

The second half of the narrative, with its grisly images of amputations and drownings, has always terrified Christians. We are not at all sure what sort of offenses of the eye are so heinous that you would have to tear one out, but we fear that the little, hidden things we do (eating quarts of ice cream in secret, pulling alongside a city bus to have a better look at an underwear ad) will turn out to be big capital sins when we stand before the seat of judgment. And, after all, there really is no getting around the fact that the text tells us, literally, to cut off our hands and tear out our eyes. Surely this is a passage about personal sinfulness!

What is really at issue in this part of the text, however, is the second of Mark's community concerns: defection from within. And only one kind of "sinner" is singled out: the person who causes the "little ones" to stumble. Still reading for the literal sense, two key words in this verse are *mikroi*, the "little ones," and *skandalizontai*, "to cause to stumble" or "to trip up," from which we get our verb "to scandalize." *Mikroi* can also be translated as "the least," or even as "children," but it carries the connotation of "the weak" as well. These people are not the physically weak, however, nor even the innocent, but those who have less fortitude for the demands of discipleship. In Mark, the verb *skandalizontai* is a technical term that means to cause to fall from the way of the cross, to stumble off the road, to abandon discipleship. In short, "to scandalize the little ones" is to apostasize oneself or cause another to do so. What this text reveals, then, is the very serious problem of community erosion.

What about the historical context of this passage? Mark's people, living in the midst of the Jewish-Roman war, were assaulted on all sides, perhaps even persecuted on all sides. They may have suffered at the hands of the Romans because of their subversive political rhetoric. They may have suffered at the hands of the Jewish leadership because of their subversive religious rhetoric. And for the insurrectionist groups, Mark's brand of revolutionary rhetoric—by losing your life you can gain it—must have looked deeply subversive to the goals of Davidic nationalism (8:34-37). Pressed on all sides, some members of Mark's community probably stumbled from the way, and still others may actually have betrayed the *mikroi* to their various enemies. So collapse of community was an urgent matter.

In order to stress the seriousness of the crisis, Jesus uses the images of amputation to urge the community to remove offending members from its midst. Just as some ancient communities literally cut off the hands of thieves, so the sacred community must figuratively cut off the hand of treachery laid to its "body." These are unsettling metaphors, but Mark believes that strong images are appropriate to intolerable sins. In fact, this is the only place in his entire gospel where Mark makes allusion to eschatological judgment, and that judgment is brought to bear only on a pair of sins: falling from the community of faith and, far worse, being the occasion of someone else's fall from faithfulness.

In the end, however, forgiveness is available even for unforgivable sins, as the final verses of Mark's passage reveal: "Have salt in yourselves, and be at peace with one another" (9:49). To bring *salt* and *fire* together here symbolically highlights healing and reconciliation as the ultimate community ethic. Physicians in the ancient world seem to have closed amputation wounds by the application of salt and fire, while the Hebrew Bible speaks of sealing a covenant with salt (see Numbers 18:19). So woundedness is healed by fire and to share salt at table is to be in fellowship. And there is no savor to a meal that is not fired and salted with peace.

In my reading of this text so far, I have concentrated on its literal and historical meanings. It is important, however, not to neglect a prophetic reading too, because Mark here says a number of important things about what it means to be church. First of all, while the boundaries of the believing community must be clearly drawn, they must also be fluid. We Christians must be unambiguous about our identity as faithful people, but this clarity is not meant to exclude. A ministry of compassion draws people in, it does not push them out. And it draws in unconditionally: "Yes, but. . ." is not a formula of baptismal welcome. One of the most significant issues of community formation for the church today is how we view our relationship to outsiders, especially those who are different from us. Mark is unequivocal on the matter: the discipleship community welcomes the stranger. He makes this point clearly through Jesus' saying: "Whoever gives you a cup of water to drink because you bear the name of Christ will by no means lose the reward" (9:41). In other words, "insiders" are very likely to find themselves on the receiving end of grace from "outsiders."

Second, membership has consequences. It demands faithfulness to the Way, faithfulness to the gospel message, and faithfulness to living out the demands of discipleship. The terms are non-negotiable. Like it or not, there are clear expectations of community members. One expectation is that we must be held accountable to the promises of the covenant of baptism: sins like sexism and racism, for example, betray the baptismal promise to "respect the dignity of every human being" (BCP 305); they must be named for the sins they are and repented. Sometimes, however, we evade the demands of the gospel by invoking a liberal tolerance that seeks to accommodate individual behavior lest it offend individual autonomy. But liberal tolerance can also offend the gospel; individual autonomy is not a Christian virtue. Quite the contrary. As Augustine of Hippo noted centuries ago, it is not that community is formed by what we bring to it, but that we are formed by what we take from it. A Christian is not self-defined.

This passage also reminds us that the church must try to resolve conflicts and seek unity, and if not unity then at least a plurality salted with peace. Neither can be achieved without forgiveness, so forgiveness must be the core of community life. It must also be its defining border. The unforgiving member stands not only outside the boundaries of community, but outside the boundaries of grace as well.

∾ "Because of Your Hardness of Heart"

In addition to wondering about the character of their new common life, early followers of Jesus naturally had questions about how that life ought to be ordered day to day. Individual choice, after all, does affect the life of the community, so it is not surprising that the gospels pay some attention to personal moral quandaries such as the matter of divorce. Few churches these days shun the divorced parishioner, but to put asunder what God has joined together still occasions high ethical anxiety among Christians. Much of the anxiety stems from what we *think* the Bible's position is by taking its pronouncements out of context or not taking the time to study with care the nuanced details of a text. To understand better the Bible's position on divorce, let us see what Jesus says about it in Matthew 19:1-9 and Mark 10:2-12. As you read these parallel accounts, note how they seem to vary only slightly; but the minor variations are significant.

The last verse of Matthew's account of Jesus' debate with the Pharisees seems to be unambiguous: divorce and remarriage are equivalent to adultery. And Mark appears to underscore that conclusion in verse 10:12. Nonetheless, I think that the core issue is not a more rigorous definition of adultery, but a more egalitarian definition of relationship. The question posed to Jesus by the Pharisees—"Is it lawful for a man to divorce his wife for any cause?" (19:3)—could as easily have been posed: "Under what *conditions* is it lawful?" Either way, the focus is exclusively on the male partner. Since Jewish family law did not recognize reciprocity for women, the debate among the rabbis was framed only in terms of which causes were sufficient for a man to "dismiss" his wife. One was adultery. When Mary is "found to be with child," for example, Joseph—before he knows that the conception is of the Holy Spirit—first plans "to dismiss her quietly" or, as it is more quaintly phrased in the *King James Version*, "put her away privily" (Matthew 1:18-21). In the ancient world, betrothal was more or less equivalent to marriage, and certainly the writ of promise was as binding. Joseph thought he was about to receive damaged goods in what was essentially a property transaction, so he was within his legal rights to seek a "divorce." It took the counsel of an angelic messenger in a dream to soften his "hardness of heart."

Thus, Jesus' words to the disciples as recorded in Mark's version—"Whoever divorces his wife and marries another commits adultery *against her*" (Mark 9:11, emphasis added)—would have stunned his original hearers. He makes a bold adjustment to the ordering of relationships between men and women; that a man could commit adultery against his wife was a possibility not even considered in ancient Judaism, where everyone understood—including the wives—that women were sexual property. He could commit adultery against another *man*, and that man's wife could be held accountable for her part in the sexual misadventure, but it was always the man, never the woman, who was the offended party. So here Jesus is leveling the playing field. Indeed, now the woman even has rights to initiate divorce ("And if she divorces her husband"), which goes far beyond the original Mosaic teaching. I suspect that Jesus understood divorce as a deeply regrettable step, a relational and spiritual tragedy, but even so, justice and equity must not be abandoned when taking it. Therefore both parties to the marriage can bring proceedings for its dissolution and both must take responsibility for its failure.

Matthew, you may have noticed, is not so bold as Mark in reordering the marital relationship. He omits, for example, Mark's provision that a woman can also divorce her husband and adds the single disclaimer that one presumably *can* divorce on the grounds of sexual infidelity (see 5:32). Note that Matthew is here no more egalitarian than the Pharisees in placing the burden of adultery on the woman, not the man. He does not say that the *man* commits adultery, but that he makes the *woman* an adulteress by divorcing her; and it is the divorced status of the woman that occasions adultery on remarriage! I suspect Matthew wants to mute what in Mark is really a very radical teaching. As we will discover below in chapter 7, Matthew works harder than any other gospel writer to place Jesus in continuity with Jewish tradition, rather than have him seem to break precipitously from it. So I think Mark's teaching on divorce is simply too novel for Matthew to embrace fully, and he reshapes it so as to be less startling for Jewish readers. He moves the tradition along, but not so far as does Mark.

Both writers, however, have Jesus locate his teachings on divorce within the context of ancient Hebrew scripture. The idea of mutuality can be traced, says Jesus, to the first chapter of the book of Genesis, where it is written that "male and female he created them" (1:27). The full verse from which Jesus quotes is actually three lines of Hebrew poetry:

> And created God humankind in his image;
> in the image of God created he him;
> male and female he created them.

The first two lines of the poem introduce its central idea: humanity is created in the image of God. Note that the last three words of the first line are repeated in the first three words of the second. This repetition creates an emphasis that you can see better when the overlapping lines are italicized:

> And created/God humankind/*in-his-image*
> *In-the-image*-of/God/created he him

"God's image," if you will, is the pivot point of the poem. But to get the meaning of "image of God," you have to look closely at the second and third lines as well.

> *In the image of God*/created/he him
> *male and female*/created/he them

Note that these lines have parallel structures in their nouns, verb, and pronouns; and the most strikingly parallel is "male and female" in line three set below "image of God" in line two. In the structure of the poem the former defines the latter: that is, what the first pair of lines emphasizes, the second pair interprets. Thus male and female *are* the image of God. Of course, male and female do not fully explicate the meaning; no single revelation of God ever begins to exhaust the inexhaustible. Still, the poem does say that at a minimum the nature of God includes these two things: male and female.

Also note that I am not making here a theological argument, but a literary one. In this instance, the character of the God of the Bible is revealed by analysis of the specific structures of one of its earliest poetic writings. That analysis adds another item to our developing list of reading strategies, the literary-critical method.

What is most intriguing, however, is a further movement in the poem, this time from singular to plural pronouns:

In the image of God/created/he *him*
male and female/created/he *them*

God the creator is singular (that is, *him*), while God's created image is plural (that is, *them*). Old Testament scholar
Phyllis Trible argues that the use of the plural indicates the
creation of distinct realities within the divine singular: humanity was not originally androgynous and then split
into two conflicting sexualities; rather, male and female
were created as different but harmonious, not opposing,
sexes.[1] Such a reading rules out sexual hierarchy. Created
simultaneously and equally, neither male nor female has
power over the other. This, I think, is the equity of power
that Jesus assigns to both partners in marriage and divorce
when he addresses the Pharisees on the topic.

There are actually two creation poems in Genesis, and
Jesus quotes from the second as well (Genesis 2:4-25). Actually, he conflates 2:24 and 1:27! Some of the details of
Genesis 2 have long been taken to imply the superiority of
men and the subordination of women: woman is fashioned from the rib of man; he is made first and she comes
out of his side. Moreover, God's motive for creating her
seems to be that Adam is overburdened by the tending of
Eden; so, says God, "I will make him a helper fit for him"
(2:18), which sounds more like patriarchy than parity.
The *New Revised Standard Version* attempts to solve the
problem by translating the verse, "I will make him a helper
as his partner." That translation begins to move us in the

---

1. I draw my interpretation of this text largely from her book *God and
   the Rhetoric of Sexuality* (Philadelphia: Fortress Press, 1987).

direction of a more adequate reading of the literal sense of the text, because while the English word "helper" carries the connotation of a subordinate assistant, the Hebrew original (`ezer*) is never used anywhere in Scripture to designate an inferior. In fact, it is often used to speak of Yahweh as the savior of Israel.

In her analysis of Genesis 2, however, Trible points out the striking similarity between the Hebrew word for man (*'adam*) and the one for the dust out of which he is formed (*ha-'adamâ*); the first is probably a pun on the second. Thus, Trible argues that "earth creature" is a better translation for what we have been content to render as "Adam." After the creation of *'adam*, God acts to differentiate this earth creature into male (*ish*) and female (*isha*). Divine reflection convinces him that the animals, which have been tried and found wanting, are not suitable companions for *'adam*. Thus it is humanity and sexuality that are created in succession, not male and female. Furthermore, it is humanity that is superior to the animals, not woman who is inferior to man. By this reading, the second creation account in Genesis describes the unity that is within sexual difference.

So if the creation narrative in Genesis 1 presents mutuality between the sexes as an ethical ideal, the text in chapter 2 affirms partnership as a relational ideal. Indeed, just before God proposes to make the earth creature a "helper," he assesses the solitariness of *'adam* and concludes, "It is not good" (Genesis 2:18). This is the only time in the creation accounts where God surveys his work and judges it to be inadequate, which supports the idea of sacred companionability as fundamental to the relationship between men and women.

In the end, I would argue that we should read this passage about divorce for its prophetic sense—not as a set of

legal directives but as an icon for the sacramental character of all relationships within the believing community.
That, in fact, is what I think Jesus is actually doing here.
While the Pharisees are anxious about how to read a specific point of the law—believing that its strict observance is
essential for holiness—Jesus gathers together pieces of the
larger biblical tradition in order to explore the more fundamental character of holiness in relationships. By giving
pride of place to the creation narratives of Genesis over the
stipulations of Mosaic law, Jesus is rereading, reassembling, and reappropriating his own sacred texts.

Historically, Christians have read the texts of our ethical tradition more like the Pharisees than like Jesus. In our
rush to relieve the anxiety of our moral quandaries, we
have tended to miss the forest for the trees. Concerning the
sacrament of marriage, for example, we have usually focused on the ideal of fidelity and neglected those of mutuality and companionability, forgetting that all three must
exist for marriage to be sacramental. A sacrament, of
course, is not something conferred, but something lived.
The blessing of the church does not create a sacrament, but
merely endorses one already made. Thus, when mutuality
and companionability are absent, the sacramental life of a
marriage has died even though fidelity may live on; divorce has already occurred and hardness of heart has already set in. Legal writs of dissolution only name that
truth. A prophetic reading of this passage on divorce,
therefore, tells us less about the contractual obligations of
marriage and more about the covenantal character of all
God-centered relationships: it tells us that these must be
marked by faithfulness, mutuality, and companionship.

～ Life at the Edges: Eschatology and Ethics

There is one more dimension of the New Testament's contribution to forming community character that we need to examine, and that is the legacy of St. Paul. An important rule of thumb for reading Paul is that his ethics reflect his eschatology: they are worked out in expectation of the end of the world as we know it and the dawning of the reign of God. Consider *his* recommendations concerning marriage, which you will find in 1 Corinthians 7:25-29a, 32-35.

Paul begins and ends this passage with a disclaimer. He is not laying down the law; he has an "opinion" to offer, not a "command of the Lord" to impose. Thus by his own admission Paul does not dictate ethical strictures, but offers counsel on community character. What is most important, however, is that Paul's advice is superimposed on his expectation of "the impending crisis" (7:26). The crisis is the coming of the end time, the *eschaton*. Like many of his contemporaries, Paul lived in anticipation of an immediate apocalyptic end to the world and the coming of the kingdom. He saw his world perched on the very edge of God's in-breaking and radical transformation. Consequently all of life is to be ordered by this apocalyptic expectation, and ordinary matters merely distract the believer from preparing for the new reality. Marriage, for example, was a distraction. To give Paul's advice a modern ring, how can you focus on being ready for the kingdom if the mortgage is in arrears and the kids need orthodontia? And if these mundane concerns divert one's focus, sexual passions are even more problematic. This is why Paul advised the Corinthians to remain in whatever state they found themselves. Sex was not sinful, just irrelevant.

Within a short half-century after Paul's death, however, the early believing communities began to realize that the second coming had been delayed, and the church settled in for the long haul. Today most Christians are still not a particularly apocalyptic people. So before we embrace unilaterally all of Paul's ethical teachings as normative, we need to reflect carefully on his world-view. There is one point, however, where Paul's world and ours ought to coincide, and that is in six verses of splendid advice on the nature of community character eloquently set forth in 1 Corinthians 13:8-13.

To begin with a historical reading of this well-known passage, the church at Corinth was made up largely of a group of converts from Eastern mystery religions who appear to have been a fairly fractious lot. Much of Paul's letter is devoted to issues that were divisive among them: economic and social status, how to celebrate the liturgy, traditions borrowed from their former pagan cults. It is also clear that some members, jockeying for positions of leadership, had certain attributes they considered evidence of special connection to the divine—gifts of the spirits, if you will. Among these were an ability to discern the future, which Paul calls "prophecy"; a kind of esoteric wisdom, which he calls "knowledge"; and an inclination toward ecstatic utterance in church, called "tongues."

Having moved from pagan cult to Christian faith, the Corinthians quite naturally thought that their old abilities were now new signs of election by the Holy Spirit. The problem, however, was that the gifts gave rise to a competitive atmosphere. Some gifts seemed so extraordinary that their recipients assumed an air of superiority. Others not so fortunate felt discontented about the quality of their gifts. Still others wondered if they had received any gift at all. The difficulty was that every course of action, supposedly an action of the Spirit, became little more than self-validation. The charisma of the gifted had less to do with an authentic movement of the Holy Spirit and more to do with the importance of being "me." That was decidedly *not* the egalitarian ethic Paul wanted in his churches—or that Jesus teaches in the gospels.

But the larger issue in the passage is Paul's conviction that the celebration of particular gifts and individual gift-edness betrays an inadequate eschatology, a poor under-standing of a world that *he* knew was radically changed. Paul says, in effect, that when you single out your particular charism as evidence that you have "arrived," you do not appreciate the crisis that is pending.

Elsewhere in the letter, Paul talks about those of us who live as heirs of the gospel as living at "the edges [or *ends*] of the ages" (10:11). There are two edges and two ages.[2] The first is the trailing edge of the *old age*, the historical sweep that concluded with the crucifixion. The second is the lead-ing edge of the *new age*, which is the consummation of all things—the *parousia*, in the Greek, the establishment of the reign of God. Although not yet fully realized, its begin-nings are revealed by the resurrection. Paul distinguishes between these two ages by reference to the fragmentary and the full: "But when the complete comes, the partial will come to an end" (13:9). In the specific instance of the crisis at Corinth, Paul talks about the old and the new in terms of gifts, which are transient, and love, which is per-manent. Because love is the defining character of the age to come, it will never fail; because the gifts are of the age that is passing away, they will also pass away.

Verses 8 through 12 of the text make this point. First, the Corinthian gifts—prophecies, tongues, and knowl-edge—are named in order (vv. 8b, 8c, 8d). Each gift is then linked to a term that designates the charism as belonging

---

2. The Greek is clearly plural for both nouns. Some translations avoid *lectio difficile* by rendering "edges" as singular: "the edge of the ages."

to the *old age* (vv. 9, 11a, 12a), and each of these is juxtaposed with a word or phrase that signifies the character of the *new age* (vv. 10, 11b, 12b). As the verses of the passage unfold, Paul's assessment of each of the gifts is revealed against the background of his eschatology. But that is probably easiest to see if we lay out the key words side-by-side, as in the following table.

	The Old Age	*The New Age*
A. prophecies (v. 8b)	the partial (v. 9)	the full (v. 10)
B. tongues (v. 8c)	the child (v. 11a)	the man (v. 11b)
C. knowledge (v. 8d)	dim mirror (v. 12a)	face to face (v. 12b)

What we have here, I think, is Paul's brilliant exposé of individual charismatic behaviors in the light of his eschatological perspective. Prophecies are of the old by virtue of their partial revelatory character; tongues, because they are of the nature of things of the child; and knowledge, because it gives an understanding of God that is at best enigmatic, like looking at something through opaque glass.

I think Paul believes that all behavior should be measured according to this eschatology. But here is the catch! The edges of the ages actually overlap precisely because the old has not yet given way completely to the new. The signs of resurrection are everywhere, but so are the signs of crucifixion. Paul was both a visionary and a realist. Thus, he understood that faithful people live in the "right now" *and* the "not yet," in the space that I call "funky time." Everything looks quite ordinary and familiar—and maybe even a little down and dirty. But there is also a bright edge of

novelty, promise, and excitement to the grit; there are diamonds among the dust. No wonder the Corinthians were
confused. It is not easy when you have to make decisions
about day-to-day behavior and still remain faithful to a
future not fully revealed.

I think Paul understood this difficulty, which is why he
backed off from being a legislator of morals in favor of being an adviser on character. On the whole, his advice is that
those behaviors that tend toward the love that gathers in
should be favored, and those that tend toward the gifts
that single out should be shunned. But he does not go
much beyond that general distinction in providing his
churches with specific moral direction. Paul says that one
should move from patterns of life that crucify to those that
raise up. But discerning the difference is difficult, and it
only happens when the community is in an ongoing conversation about its character. If you live at the edges of the
ages, ethics have to be interrogatory and dialogical rather
than proscriptive and foreclosed. There are no simple rules
to follow, only questions with which to wrestle.

In the end, Holy Scripture does not give us answers to
the problems we face: urban poverty or public education
for illegal immigrants, global warming or wetlands recla-
mation, euthanasia or the allocation of limited health care
resources, teenage pregnancy or premarital sex. But it does
provide a character for the believing community out of
which we can have theological conversations around our
social issues. Likewise, we need to remember that the Bible
does not announce itself as the Word of God; that is our attribution. So our sacred texts are not the final word on
God's preferred behavior for us. In fact, our behavior, like
our faith, draws on a Person, not a Book, however sacred
that Book has come to be. The Person asks us to reflect on
our points of moral anxiety along the greater arc of an

ethic of love. Neither he, nor his perhaps most eloquent apostle, do the sums of our ethical arithmetic. But they both invite us into an ongoing conversation about what kind of community we are called to be "in the meantime."

Chapter 6

Who is the God of the Bible?

Somewhere in my library is a little book of cartoons called *Things Children Say About God*. One I remember particularly shows a little girl looking up at a parent and asking, "Is Fr. Brown a friend of God, or does he just know Him through business?" Behind that question—which is also an amusing indictment of the religious "professional" who may or may not be on familiar terms with God—is the more urgent and poignant yearning all of us have to know who God is. And particularly, who is the God we are supposed to know from the pages of the Bible?

It takes a lot of confidence for any author even to begin to answer that question. But I want to wrestle with it here because, phrased in a variety of ways, it is the question I am most frequently asked by groups of Bible readers. The second is "Who is Jesus?", which is the topic of the next chapter. I do not pretend to offer a succinct yet comprehensive biblical theology; in fact, I do not believe we can articulate any such thing. The attempt to be both succinct and comprehensive can make for shallow reading and leave us with a God who is only one thing: wisdom or love or justice or mercy or judgment. It also avoids the tensions we find on the pages of the Bible itself, where God appears to embrace one of those virtues, say compassion, in one text and then assumes an altogether different posture in another. In short, a single hermeneutic will not do. God may be a single, comprehensive reality in heaven, but the God we find in most of the biblical texts—who actually seems to have some "shadow" sides as well—is busy and restless, an innovative Creator who is working some very strange sides of the streets of the world.

Part of the problem of trying to pin down the God of the Bible to any single attribute of deity is that the narratives themselves have been collected over thousands of years—and written, rethought, edited, and edited again by probably hundreds of storytellers, authors, and scribes. The various writings of the Hebrew Bible, for example, bear witness to the unique history of a particular people with their Yahweh from the time of the beginning of the nation of Israel, shortly after the year 2000 B.C.E., and running down through the Maccabean Revolt, which broke out about a hundred and fifty years before the birth of Jesus. That, to put it mildly, is sufficient time for the vagaries of cultural and social change to provide an enormous spectrum of reflections on the nature of God.

Some have taken the cynical view that the so-called religious experiences of biblical record have been manufactured out of human feelings and imagination; that is, we have simply made up God as we have gone along. I prefer to think that God's variety, ambiguity, nuance, and contradiction come honestly from people's authentic experience of God in concrete and diverse situations. In this incarnational stance the divine and the human are both involved in the ongoing work of creation, so God makes *us* up as we go along as much as we make up God! I am also very cautious about dispensing too quickly with human feelings and imagination as legitimate playing fields for the Divine; it is always chancy to underestimate how hard the Spirit of God drives our imagination! Just such a spirit seems to have driven the imagination of the prophet Isaiah in his vision of God:

> In the year that King Uzziah died, I saw the Lord sitting on a throne, high and lofty; and the hem of his robe filled the temple. Seraphs were in attendance above him; each had six wings: with two they covered their faces, and with two they covered their feet, and with two they flew. And one called to another and said: "Holy, holy, holy is the LORD of hosts; the whole earth is full of his glory." The pivots of the threshold shook at the voices of those who called, and the house filled with smoke. (Isaiah 6:1-4)

"Holy, holy, holy, Lord God of hosts." Those are very familiar words, recited by every worshiper each time we sing or say the *Sanctus* in the eucharist, and they come from this vision of Isaiah.[1] But what does the prophet really mean by "holy"? Tracing backward from the Latin *sanctus*, through the Greek *hagios*, gives the Hebrew word *kaddosh*, which means "otherness," a radical separation. So the seraphs in Isaiah's vision are actually crying, "Yahweh is other! other! other!" This is a deity, awesome, numinous, and presidential, who occupies a reality vastly different from our own. He is attended by a pair of angelic beings who cover their faces lest they look upon his. At the sound of their voices, the whole temple seems to shift on its foun-

---

1. The Rite II version replaces "Lord God of hosts" with "God of power and might," an attempt to define the meaning of "glory." The Greek word is *doxa*, which carries a sense that does not translate easily; roughly it means "weight," "splendor," or "radiance."

dations. And Yahweh is engulfed, like the God of Mount Sinai who hides his face from Moses, in a cloud of smoke.

That is a very different deity from the one we find recorded in Hosea 11:1-4:

When Israel was a child, I loved him,
   and out of Egypt I called my son.
The more I called them,
   the more they went from me;
they kept sacrificing to the Baals,
   and offering incense to idols.
Yet it was I who taught Ephraim to walk,
   I took them up in my arms;
   but they did not know that I healed them.
I led them with cords of human kindness,
   with bands of love.
I was to them like those
   who lift infants to their cheeks.
I bent down to them and fed them.

The God of this text, neither too great nor too marvelous, is not shrouded in a cloud of mystery beyond reach; this is a divine presence very close at hand. In fact, the God of this passage takes your infant hands in his and steadies your halting first steps, raises you up when you fall, and cuddles you cheek to cheek. Luke 13:34 calls this God a mother hen gathering her chicks under her wings.

I do not think for a minute that these two images are contradictory; in fact, one complements the other. There is no single metaphor, nor complex of metaphors, that serves fully to define the ineffable character of God. No single revelation can exhaust all that is to be revealed. In fact, the more adept you become at the kind of critical Bible reading I have tried to suggest in these pages, the more you begin to see that the God of the biblical tradition is not a single reality at all, but a multiplicity of realities, a diversity, more a plurality than a unity—and often uncomfortably so. As Walter Brueggemann, one of our best contemporary biblical scholars, puts it, "The problem for the God of the Bible is that the God of the Bible is a Jew, and the Jews are a very unsettled people. So what you get from them is a very unsettled God."[2]

What Brueggemann has in mind are texts like Exodus 34:6, where Yahweh says to Moses, "The LORD, the LORD, a God merciful and gracious, slow to anger, and abounding in steadfast love and faithfulness, keeping steadfast love for the thousandth generation, forgiving iniquity and transgression and sin." But immediately, in verse 7, God provides a startlingly different self-disclosure as the one who will by no means clear the guilty, but will visit "the iniquity of the parents upon the children and the children's children, to the third and the fourth generation." Brueggemann observes that when Moses discovers God has both a Plan A and a Plan B in mind, he falls on his face and cries out, "Oh Lord, implement Plan A!"

There are all sorts of texts like these that disclose God's rich, unsettled, and lively interiority that cannot, *must* not, be reduced to a single, one-dimensional reading. Indeed, God's biography is so complicated that to get any sense of the God revealed in our sacred stories, you almost have to move through them one text at a time. And as you do, you will come to encounter a God who is more sublimely complex than you would ever have thought before.

---

2. Walter Brueggemann, "God's Otherness and our Othering," a lecture given at the 25th National Conference of Trinity Institute, January 25, 1994.

~ The God Who Will Not Sit Still

Let us start by simply admitting up front that no single or "settled" interpretive approach will fully reveal the unsettled, restless, Semitic God of the Bible. Still, given that disclaimer, I think it *is* possible to identify—especially when you pay attention to the historical context out of which the authors of the Hebrew scriptures wrote—a threefold movement in the development of their doctrine of God.[3] Consider first a text from Joshua: chapter 1, verses 1-6.

As you read those verses, ask yourself what kind of god is revealed by the literal sense of this text. What I think emerges is essentially a tribal deity: God chooses the children of Israel above all other tribes and provides the land on which to secure their ethnic identity. This theme of election and provision runs through much of Israel's myth of origins—from Yahweh's promise to Abraham that his offspring will become a great nation to the conquest of Canaan. And on the eve of that conquest, as this passage tells us, the character of the relationship between Yahweh and his tribe is reaffirmed.

The boundaries of the land promised to Joshua are unclear, although they are variously sketched in three separate sources (Numbers 34:1-12; Joshua 13:1-7; Ezekiel 47:13-20), each of which carves out a fairly large piece of turf, much of it outside Palestine. These biblical "maps" probably visualized the past in light of King David's epic conquests, which did extend much of Israel's territorial possessions. The original area was small, however, and

---

3. What follows is owed in part to Fr. Naim Ateek, the pastor of the Arab congregation of St. George's Cathedral in Jerusalem, and to his book *Justice and Only Justice: A Palestinian Theology of Liberation* (New York: Orbis Books, 1989).

hard won at that—as the book of Judges makes clear when it reveals that the occupation project was never as thoroughgoing nor successful as the book of Joshua would have you believe. For example, the ancient Israelites never succeeded in displacing the Philistines from the Mediterranean coast—and thus never acquired as part of the "promise" that strip of coastal plain where the population density of modern Israel is greatest. (Which is why you hear religious Jews today saying, "So what is Tel Aviv?!") In short, the tribes of ancient Israel occupied a relatively small parcel of land consisting of what is now Judea, Samaria, most of the Galilee, and a parallel strip of hill country east of the Jordan River. When you read through the accounts given in the book of Joshua, it becomes clear that securing even that little piece of property involved an almost ceaseless struggle to subdue the indigenous peoples. And over the struggle presided a God of single-minded purpose, who watches over the Israelites' battles, beginning with the bloody siege of Jericho (Joshua 6:1-21).

By contrast, consider the God of a passage from the book of the prophet Micah, one of the most stirring in all the Hebrew Bible. In Micah 4:1-4, God lays aside his armor and bids the nations to do so, too. He not only abandons warfare but overturns the ethnocentric claims of a singular people to a particular piece of turf. This God favors a people who will cultivate a land into which all humanity might peacefully flow.

Micah's career appears to have spanned the events surrounding the Assyrian conquest of the northern kingdom of Israel, roughly 720-700 B.C.E. However, a reference (4:10) to the subsequent Babylonian captivity of Judah, the southern kingdom (587-538 B.C.E.), indicates that Micah's original oracles were updated and expanded in the post-exilic period. Perhaps when a restored nation came to reflect on its new identity in light of the exile, one of the voices from the past that helped reassemble its story for the present—and its understanding of its Yahweh—was Micah's, heard calling a people who had now twice been subdued and oppressed to abandon their own chauvinistic habits of conquest and oppression. Actually, Micah's voice is not the only one to have spoken; the prophetic writers consistently challenged the older and narrower idea of God as a tribal deity. Isaiah too, for example, speaks of a God who turns swords into plowshares and spears into pruning hooks (2:4).

There is a third reading of God that comes out of the legal tradition of Hebrew scripture, a God who leads the Israelites into more ethical and justice-seeking paths, especially in their treatment of outsiders. The legal code found in the book of Deuteronomy, for example, forbids an Ammonite or a Moabite to enter the assembly of the Lord, even to the tenth generation (23:3), but it also commands the Israelites, "You shall not abhor any of the Edomites, for they are your kin. You shall not abhor any of the Egyptians, because you were an alien residing in their land" (23:7). The Jewish ethic of hospitality is particularly clear in passages such as Deuteronomy 24:17-18, in which Yahweh's people are told, "You shall not deprive a resident alien or an orphan of justice; you shall not take a widow's garment in pledge. Remember that you were a slave in Egypt and the LORD your God redeemed you from there; therefore I command you to do this." Here Israel is instructed to remember the Exodus not as a mandate for conquest—in fact, there is no explicit promise of the land in the Exodus narrative itself—but as a reason for generosity. In fact, the theme of hospitality, as opposed to hostility, is at the root of Hebrew tradition. When Abraham and Sarah offered hospitality to a set of strangers in their tent at

Mamre, it turned out they were entertaining angels un-awares—messengers of God who announced the pending birth of Isaac, the son of their barrenness and old age (Genesis 18:1-15). The promise to Israel was thus born out of generosity to the foreign.

This God who shows concern for all humanity emerges also in one of my favorite Old Testament passages from Amos, verse 7 of chapter 9. The God of this passage reminds the Israelites that while they have been subjects of his liberating action, they have not been alone: he has also brought up Israel's long-standing adversaries from the land of *their* enemies—the Philistines from Caphtor, the Arameans, or Syrians, from Kir, and, by implication in the opening phrase, the Ethiopians as well. Here God seems to say, "Look, I'm not denying that your Exodus was a really big deal. But I do it *all* the time. That's just the sort of God I am."[4]

I have to admit that in my presentation of these three dimensions of God's reality, I have stacked the deck. It may seem from this that the God of the Bible is "in process," undergoing a positive transformation from primitive tribal warrior to proclaimer of social justice to universalist moral guide. The truth is that all three ways of looking at God are layered throughout the Hebrew tradition. Even the passage from Amos is located within a longer monologue—a diatribe, really—of a very angry and judging God, the voice of vengeance and violence not yet completely silenced. But the God of social justice with an ethic of inclusivity is particularly compelling for modern believers. We have a strong aversion to religious faith expressed through militarism and territorial claims, so we like the idea of a God who has been in process. However, lest we

---

4. Brueggemann, "God's Otherness and our Othering."

turn the God of the Bible into a western liberal, we had better look at some other texts. There are a few surprises in store.

∼ Who's in Charge Here?

One of the things I like about the more surprising texts of the Bible is that they are often so playful in their ambiguities. Sometimes you cannot even sort out which character is playing God and which one is playing humanity. The story in which Abraham bargains with God over the fate of Sodom and Gomorrah is just such a passage, Genesis 18:22-33. Take time to read it now.

God has been aware of the sin of Sodom for some time and decides on an executive, onsite inspection. But just before departure, Abraham sidles up and says, "Listen, you don't mean to destroy the whole place, do you? Must the righteous suffer with the wicked? What if it turns out that there are, say, fifty decent folk there?" To which God says, "Well, I hadn't really thought about it like that. All right, if I find fifty righteous, I will spare the place for their sake. Far be it from me to slay the righteous with the wicked!" Emboldened by his success, Abraham ups the ante: "Listen, how about forty-five?" And so forth.

The God of this text is not a justice-minded western liberal but a Middle Eastern rug merchant. Anyone who has bartered in a market in the Middle East can recognize the situation. A pair of malachite earrings in a shop window catches your eye, so you go in. The owner joins you in admiring the craftsmanship, and you inquire about the price. He confides they are worth some astronomical sum, but he will give you his "best price," which is, of course, way more than you intended to spend. When you wince, he lowers his price somewhat. You counteroffer; he winces. And back and forth it goes. Unable to settle, you move toward the door. Then the shopkeeper invites you to share a glass of tea, and the bargaining continues during exchanges of sociability: you learn about each other's children, commiserate about the value-added tax, and discover that the shopkeeper has a sister in Cleveland. This is also the character of Middle Eastern political diplomacy; peace treaties are negotiated this way.

Abraham knows the routine so well that he eventually wears God down. "How about forty? Will you give me forty?" "Okay, I'll give you forty." And on and on it goes until God is so worn out by Abraham's skill, by his shameless persistence, that he "went his way." The antecedent to that pronoun is ambiguous. Whose way does God go? Abraham's? God's? Who is the shopkeeper and who is the tourist in this story?

Those questions raise, I think, some critical theological issues. The entire story of Abraham is structured to highlight the faithfulness of Abraham and Sarah and the waywardness of the rest of humanity. The story of the destruction of Sodom (Genesis 19:1-29), placed within that larger epic, articulates the consequences of disobedience: those who ignore the righteousness of God will surely die when the brimstone of apocalyptic judgment rains down. Unhappily, a few of the just will fall with the unjust. Abraham protests that equation and asks God to consider a different calculus. What we seem to have here is role reversal: Abraham conceives of an alternate vision and he passes it on to God.[5]

When we look at the literal meaning of the text, we see that the story opens with Abraham standing before God,

---

5. Walter Brueggemann notes that the text sets up Abraham as if he were a professor of theology and Yahweh his student.

which is the appropriate Semitic posture for a servant in relation to his lord. But a marginal note in one of the ancient manuscripts suggests that originally the text said something like, "Yahweh stood before Abraham," which creates a totally different picture of who is in charge. Abraham presides, not God. Such a startling image must have been unacceptable to later scribes, however, who saw Yahweh as awesome and completely other. So they rewrote the story: Abraham must be accountable to God, not the other way round.

Brueggemann also points to another interesting textual detail. Twice Abraham reproaches Yahweh with the words, "Far be it from you to do such a thing" (18:25), but this is a rather weak translation. Something on the order of "That is profane!" is closer to Abraham's accusation. In other words, Abraham also presumes to instruct God that the policy of punishing the righteous along with the wicked diminishes—indeed, profanes—God's holiness. And in that instruction, the text moves beyond the issue of justice to the issue of the character of God. Abraham establishes just this connection between God's actions of justice and holiness of person: "Shall not the Judge of all the earth do what is just?" (18:25). Thus, a God who cares for the faithful few more than he despises the faithless many moves toward center stage of the biblical drama.

Not all the way, though. Sodom is still destroyed in the narrative, but Lot, the lone righteous one found, is spared (19:29). And the textual tradition never quite forgets that Yahweh, despite the rain of fire and sulfur, has made a significant ethical shift in that single saving action, prompted first by Abraham. We need to remember this story whenever we are tempted to cast God in the role of petty scorekeeper and protector of morality. God moves a long way from those postures in this text. But the remarkable thing is that Abraham leads.

~ If You Can't Bargain, Steal It!

If in one story a human being is able to reorder the theology of God's identity, in the next one God can dramatically reorder ours. Take, for example, the story of Jacob and Esau, which begins with the account of how Jacob, the younger brother, cheats the older of his birthright. It is one of the most disturbing texts in all of the Hebrew Bible, as well as the pivot point in the long Jacob epic that extends from Genesis 25:19 through 36:43. The entire Jacob story bears reading, but I recommend that you at least read the story in Genesis 27:1-29 now.

Jacob and Esau were twins, the sons of Isaac and Rebekah and the grandsons of Abraham and Sarah. As the elder, Esau was the heir of God's promise to Abraham that his offspring would become a great nation. By rights, the lineage should have been Abraham—Isaac—Esau—Eliphaz, *not* Abraham—Isaac—Jacob—Joseph. (Most of us have never heard of Esau's son Eliphaz; he is named in Genesis 36:4.) Jacob is a trickster, however, and connives to buy Esau's birthright for a bit of lentil stew (Genesis 25:29-34). Then he actually steals it by duping his blind and aged father into giving him the blessing that should have been reserved for Esau (Genesis 27). It is important to note the literal sense of the word *blessing* in this story. The blessing is not simply a pious prayer of a dying father over his surviving children; it is the patrilineal transfer of rights and property that descends, under ordinary circumstances, to the first, not the second, son.

Jacob's connivance for preferment actually began in the womb. When Rebekah delivered her children Esau came forth first, but the younger twin attempted to wedge himself out ahead. According to the text, Jacob was born "with his hand gripping Esau's heel" (25:26). Another translation is that he "supplanted" Esau. The text then says, "So he was named Jacob," which may be a pun on the Hebrew word that translates roughly "heel-sneak" or "over-reacher." And this is where the story gets really surprising, because it emerges that God has set the whole conflict in motion.

> The children struggled together within her; and she said, "If it is to be this way, why do I live?" So she went to inquire of the LORD. And the LORD said to her, "Two nations are in your womb, and two peoples born of you shall be divided; the one shall be stronger than the other, the elder shall serve the younger. (Genesis 25:22-23)

So the epic is not about Jacob and Esau, really, but about God. And it asks the reader to consider what kind of god will deliberately disrupt the established social order of relationship, hierarchy, and inheritance. For, as Walter Brueggemann writes, this is a world in which

> primogeniture is not simply one rule among many. It is the linchpin of an entire social and legal system which defines rights and privileges and provides a way around internecine disputes. But that same practice which protects the order of society is also a way of destining some to advantage and others to disadvantage. That world of privilege and denial is here disrupted by the God of blessing who will sojourn with the "low and despised" [cf., Luke 6:34]. The narrative, then, is a radically revolutionary announcement. It dares to call into question a conventional settlement of power.[6]

Here is a God who violates the world's notions of wisdom, power, preferment, and order. From the world's point of view, the Jacob epic reveals the dark and inscrutable side of God; from God's point of view, it reminds the world that "my thoughts are not your thoughts, nor are your ways my ways" (Isaiah 55:8). It is not Jacob who is so much the outrageous challenge to his world, but an outrageous God who challenges the vision we have of our own. One of the most ironic statements in the story comes at the point when the initially dubious Isaac asks the disguised Jacob, "How is it that you have found [the game] so quickly, my son?" And Jacob answers, "Because the LORD your God granted me success" (27:20). The irony is that by granting Jacob advantage over Esau, God endorses this duplicity.

Which is a reminder that we cannot pass over the role of Rebekah in this drama (27:5-17). A conventional reading aligns her in treachery with a favored, and illegitimately promoted, son. Indeed, her brilliantly contrived deceits make her the key conspirator in a plot to defraud her husband. I cannot stress too strongly how insidious her behavior would have seemed to the ancient Hebrew hearers of this story. No wife would have subverted her husband's house in this way. But a prophetic interpretation of the text is that Rebekah does not conspire with Jacob to subvert the claims of Esau; she colludes with God to subvert the claims of patriarchy. That interpretation, I think, is consistent with the opening prophecy. It was God's decision, after all, that the "elder shall serve the younger," not Rebekah's. She merely plays out the role assigned to her as mother in the conceiving, and midwife in the birthing, of a radically different social order.

---

6. Walter Brueggemann, *Genesis* (Atlanta: John Knox Press, 1982), 209.

On the pages of the New Testament, something of Rebekah's role is played by Mary of Nazareth, who also willingly colludes with God in disruption of the expected order of things. This is evident particularly in the song given to her by Luke (1:46-55) and known in Christian worship as the *Magnificat*. Although the *Magnificat* is recited every time the daily office of Evening Prayer is said or sung, Mary's perhaps more familiar words for Bible readers—uttered in response to the angel Gabriel—come just a few verses earlier in the Lucan text: "Let it be with me according to your word" (1:38). Centuries of piety have considered that single line as her character note and the model for Christian posture and behavior. Her words have been taken to reflect those virtues that culture has used both to idealize women and to hold them hostage—humility, meekness, acceptance, and obedience.

I think, however, that Mary's status is more fully developed in the powerful lines of her longer song, where she reveals herself as a co-conspirator with that restless and imaginative God who is about to accomplish a surprising reversal of all things. The arrogance of power is about to be shattered and the future given to the powerless. The lowly will be lifted up, and the exalted cast down. The hungry will be filled with good things and the rich sent away empty. There is nothing in the words of the *Magnificat* that speaks of pious obedience to business as usual. It is a song of liberation, sung in praise of the God who executes a new social order of justice and plenty.

∿ **Upside-Down Justice**

But you might begin to wonder exactly what kind of justice God has in mind when you read the parable of the widow and the unjust judge, which appears in the very same gospel as the *Magnificat* (Luke 18:1-8). The parable underscores how raucously unpredictable God can be in the New Testament as well as in the Hebrew Bible.

To begin a literal interpretation of the text we need first to isolate the story itself from Luke's introduction and Jesus' conclusion; on either side of the parable is a commentary on prayer (18:1, 6-8). For the moment, put those verses aside. Then consider the character note for the widow: her "continually coming." Clearly she did not make a single appeal to the judge; she was tirelessly persistent. Perhaps without money, influence, or an appeals process, her only recourse was to make a pest of herself.

Consider also the character of the judge. Luke says that he is not a "God-fearer" and has no scruples. Luke's gospel routinely uses the term "God-fearer" for gentiles who are attracted to Judaism. So this man is simply not religious, or not yet fully converted. His lack of "justice" may, in fact, refer to nothing more than a lack of faithfulness to the Torah. In an agricultural economy and a patriarchal culture widows were inherently vulnerable, so any judge would be well advised to take special care of them. But perhaps the widow's claim was fairly petty and the merits of the case weak, even by the standards of Torah—just the sort of nuisance plea you try to keep off your docket. Nonetheless, the judge is hearing the old woman even in his sleep. So enough is enough! He will render her a favorable verdict.

That is essentially the content of the story: a pliant judge is susceptible to a carping plaintiff. Stripped of its beginning and ending, that is not much of a story about prayer. Nonetheless, we do need to admit that Jesus does use the story to talk about prayer—or at least Luke *makes* Jesus use the story to talk about prayer! And if what Jesus is saying is that the God who responds to our prayers is like the judge, then what you have is a situation where if you nag loud enough and long enough, God will respond favorably on your behalf. In this way, the judge is reminiscent of the God who spares Lot precisely because Abraham nags him! Here again is the God with whom you can barter—but now on the pages of early Christian literature.

The God of this parable is also vaguely reminiscent of the God of the Jacob epic. Make the allegorical link, as Jesus does, between God and the judge and then ponder just what kind of God we have here. I think he is a pretty unsavory character. He neither cares what people think nor allows his conscience to move him. He is a jurist who breaks the rules of jurisprudence, a practitioner of the law who abandons its legitimate practice. He is not at all interested in rendering justice; he just wants to get this tedious widow off his back. That is not merely a God who might cave in to your skills as a bargainer, it is a God who will grant your petition just to get you to leave him alone. This God is scandalous!

But a scandal from whose perspective? Robert Farrar Capon's *The Parables of Grace*, to which I am indebted for this reading of the judge and the widow, suggests that the God of this text is an embarrassment only from *our* point of view. He is a scandal, says Capon, because he is a God who has put himself out of the judging business and into the grace business. Another way to phrase this is to say that we need to be careful about assuming that the God of the Bible necessarily agrees with our notions of what is just, right, and moral. God is not compelled to play by our rules, however exalted they might seem to us. In fact, the more I read the Bible, the more I am convinced that there is very little about God that has to do with our definitions of reasonableness and right-mindedness. It is all subversion and scandal.

For Christians, of course, scandal is where we begin—and where we end. We start with the scandalous proposition of the Incarnation; there is nothing reasonable about "a virgin shall conceive and bear a son." We end with the dead being raised, and that, when you think about it, is also a scandal. The first Easter day was an intolerable assault on a well-ordered world. Matthew says as much in his account of the post-crucifixion events.

> The next day, that is, after the day of Preparation, the chief priests and the Pharisees gathered before Pilate and said, "Sir, we remember what that imposter said while he was still alive, 'After three days I will rise again.' Therefore command the tomb to be made secure until the third day; otherwise his disciples may go and steal him away, and tell the people, 'He has been raised from the dead,' and the last deception will be worse than the first." (Matthew 27:62-64)

It would have made much better sense, as it did to the anxious Pharisees, for an empty tomb to be nothing more than a potentially embarrassing hoax. But long before the tomb was found empty, there was already the scandalous God who, like an unjust judge, confers blessings on the shrewd as well as on the sincere. Long before the stone is rolled away, the God of the Bible can be found pushing relentlessly at our fixed and stony centers with the moving and multiple edges of his life.

In the end, Isaiah has probably got it right: Yahweh is other! other! other! Which is just another way to make the point of this chapter: God has a rich and diverse interiority that no single reading can exhaust. But I think it is also a joy and comfort—*really* Good News—that the God of the Bible has some scandalous dimensions as well. Alongside wisdom and justice and love and compassion and peace,

we discover ambiguity, contradiction, and incongru-
ity—as well as some rather bad behavior. We know these
things to be true of ourselves, but we did not know them
about God. Once having made that discovery, however, we
are set free to read the stories of our own lives without
having to omit specific verses that look as if they should
not belong in our personal texts. It turns out that we may
be more in the image of our Creator than we had ever
thought.

Chapter 7

Who is the Jesus of the Bible?

As people become more adept at reading Scripture for the three senses—particularly for the literal, and paying attention to what the texts *really* say—they begin to realize that the Jesus of the Bible, just like the God of the Bible, is a many-sided figure. This realization emerges particularly when you read the gospels "horizontally" rather than "vertically," as explained by John Dominic Crossan:

> If you read those four texts vertically, as it were, from start to finish and one after another, you get a generally persuasive impression of unity, harmony, and agreement. But if you read them horizontally, focusing on this or that unit and comparing it across two, three, or four versions, it is disagreement rather than agreement that strikes one most forcibly.[1]

This discovery can be disconcerting, and sometimes it can even make people just plain angry. What makes them so furious is not the Bible itself, but the content of their re-

---

1. John Dominic Crossan, *The Historical Jesus: The Life of a Mediterranean Jewish Peasant* (San Francisco: HarperSanFrancisco, 1991), xxx.

ligious upbringing. Schooling in Christian piety has taught them that there is a single fixed view of Jesus and to think he might be otherwise is sure damnation. For many people in my Bible classes, their experience of church has been an attempt to contain Jesus, to "box him in." I do not think that the church as ever really succeeded in boxing the Savior in, but many of us have been frustrated to learn that the Jesus we learned about in Sunday school is not the complete picture.

From the time of the early church, different Christian traditions have tried to define the Christ very specifically and often on their own terms. Part of the motivation for this lies in the problems raised when you *do* read horizontally, discovering the disparate versions of Jesus in the four gospels. As early as the mid-second century, pagan opponents of Christianity, such as Celsus, and Christian apologists, such as Justin Martyr, were aware of these discrepancies, and they attempted to solve the problem of multiple accounts in one of two ways: either eliminate all the gospels save one or blend them into a single narrative. As Crossan points out, those solutions are still implicitly operative today. "Problem: there are two versions of the Lord's Prayer. Solution: cite Matthew and ignore Luke. Problem: there are two versions of Jesus' birth story. Solution: put the shepherds and the magi together at the manger."[2] By and large, Christian tradition has not encouraged horizontal reading, comparing one gospel account to another. Instead, the faithful have been taught, if they have been taught at all, to read vertically and look for agreement and unity. The result gives us a boxed-in Jesus.

In recent scholarship the lid on the box of at least the Jesus of history has been raised and the figure—more accu-

---

2. *Ibid.*

rately, the figures—that has emerged has created a good deal of anxiety about the Christ of faith in the Christian tradition. What Jesus actually said and did, and who the historical Jesus really was, are questions commanding passionate attention in our day, even in the popular press. But widespread interest in his identity as the Messiah, the Christ of faith, both human and divine, is far from new, nor has it ever been restricted to scholars. As far back as the fourth century Gregory of Nyssa, the bishop of Constantinople, records that the theological debates of his period captured the imagination even of ordinary folk.

> Garment sellers, money changers, food vendors—they are all at it. If you ask for change, they philosophize for you about generate and ingenerate natures. If you inquire about the price of bread, the answer is that the Father is greater and the Son inferior. If you speak about whether the bath is ready, they express the opinion that the Son was made out of nothing.[3]

In other words, the questions of who is the Jesus we find on the pages of the New Testament and who is the Christ of our believing tradition have always been urgent ones for the entire sacred community.

The fact that there is a distinction made at all owes in part to the discrepancies uncovered by careful reading of the Bible and to the awareness of what Bible scholars identify as at least two "voices" in the New Testament. One voice is that of the "pre-Easter Jesus of Nazareth," which some think we can "recover" through scientifically designed historical methods. This voice belongs to the Jesus of history. The other voice is that of the community of believers after Jesus' death and resurrection—the commu-

---

3. Gregory of Nyssa, *Oration on the Deity of the Son and the Holy Spirit.*

nity that reflected on the person of Jesus in theological terms, came to attribute a divine nature to him, and ultimately worshiped him as Savior and Lord. This gives us the term the Christ of faith.

John Dominic Crossan provides a useful way to think about the distinction. He argues that the Jesus tradition contains three layers. The first layer is one of retention: it is the record of the words and deeds, events and happenings, of the historical man, Jesus of Nazareth. The second layer develops that data, reflects on its meaning, and applies it to new situations, novel circumstances, and unforeseen problems. The third layer, which Crossan calls creation, involves not only the composition of new sayings and new stories but the elaboration of even larger textual complexes in which the authors are frequently making nuanced theological arguments.[4] The Jesus of history belongs to the first layer and, roughly speaking, the Christ of faith to belongs to the second and third.[5] This is not to say that the first is the only *authentic* layer while the other two are somehow invalid. Quite the contrary. Just as we discovered with the God of the Hebrew Bible, redaction of the Jesus material functioned to assist revelation. In short, the gospels are not journalistic recitations of the life of Jesus; he left behind followers who were thinkers, not merely

---

4. Crossan, *Historical Jesus*, xxxi.

5. A case in point is the bread of life discourse (John 6:1-59), which we will examine in detail in chapter 8. The text begins with the feeding of a large crowd in a deserted place. This may well represent retention; all four gospel writers agree on some version of a massive wilderness feeding as part of Jesus' ministry. But John's long theological reflection on the meaning of that miracle, including his assertion that Jesus is the true bread that feeds from heaven (6:45ff.), probably owes to development and creation.

scribes, and who believed the Christ of faith was still with them in the Holy Spirit, teaching and leading them into new truths.

Another way to understand the distinction is to ask whether the Jesus of history understood himself as the Christ of faith. Did he think of himself, for example, as the Son of God or in any sense a messianic figure? And were the messianic statements of the gospels really made by the Jesus of history, or were they placed on his lips by later Christians, including the authors of the New Testament writings themselves? When you compare examples of Jesus' sayings in the different gospel texts, you can see how questions of this sort get raised in the first place. Consider, for example, a cluster of sayings in three of the gospels about signs. Jesus is forever being asked by his opponents to trade on his relationship with the Father by providing some sign of his divine endorsement and authority. Note that in this comparison I am primarily focusing on the literal sense of each text, leaving aside the historical and prophetic for the moment—and reading horizontally.

> The Pharisees came and began to argue with him, asking him for a sign from heaven, to test him. And he sighed deeply in his spirit and said, "Why does this generation ask for a sign? Truly I tell you, no sign will be given to this generation." (Mark 8:11-12)

> When the crowds were increasing, he began to say, "This generation is an evil generation; it asks for a sign, but no sign will be given to it except the sign of Jonah. For just as Jonah became a sign to the people of Nineveh, so the Son of Man will be to this generation." (Luke 11:29-30)

> Then some of the scribes and Pharisees said to him, "Teacher, we wish to see a sign from you." But he answered them, "An evil and adulterous generation asks for a sign, but no sign will be given to it except the sign of the prophet Jonah. For just as Jonah was three days and three nights in the belly of the sea monster, so for three days and three nights the Son of Man [some sources give "son of Adam"] will be in the heart of the earth." (Matthew 12:38-40)

The single phrase shared by all three texts is the refusal of Jesus to "give a sign." In Mark, the Pharisees' request is unconditionally denied. For many scholars, that gives Mark's version high marks for historical reliability, for several reasons. First, one of the consistent characteristics of Jesus' speech in the gospels is his terse refusal to engage in verbal parry. Further, while Jesus' denial does not appear sharp in English, in the Greek it takes the form of a Hebraic oath: "May God strike me down if a sign shall be given!" The "Jewishness" of the speech tends to locate the saying within the context of the "Jewish," and thereby "historical," Jesus.

The oath disappears in Matthew and Luke, which suggests that they may have edited earlier material. In fact, Luke qualifies the denial by mentioning the sign of Jonah, drawing a parallel between Jonah as a prophet of repentance to the Ninevites and Jesus as a prophet of repentance to "this generation." So Luke's account begins to look like theological reflection on the part of the post-Easter community, particularly since one of its understandings was that Jesus had fulfilled Israel's prophetic past. In his version, Matthew takes the Jonah parallel even further so that it becomes an allusion to Jesus' death and resurrection: just as Jonah was in the belly of the great fish for three days, so will the Son of Man be in the tomb for three days. The historical Jesus might have understood his teachings on repentance to be like those of the prophet Jonah, but would he have referred to himself as "the Son of Man"? And would Jesus as "the Son of Man," self-consciously borrowing a messianic and apocalyptic title from the book of Daniel, have predicted his three-day residence in the tomb and what later came to be known as the harrowing of hell—his descent among the dead?[6] When biblical scholars come up against these kinds of textual problems, it is not difficult to see how some will argue that while Mark's version may be the actual voice of the pre-Easter Jesus, Luke's and Matthew's words are attributed to him by the post-Easter community.

That is precisely the assessment of "no sign given" made by a group of scholars known as the Jesus Seminar, which has in recent years received high-profile media coverage. Some of its members have even found themselves the unlikely subjects of cover stories in *Newsweek* and *Time* magazines and headline-makers in nationally syndicated newspapers. When, for example, the seminar pronounced in 1989 that the Lord's Prayer is unlikely to have been uttered by Jesus, the news appeared on the front page of nearly two hundred papers in the United States alone, and it looked like a frontal attack on an essential piece of Christian faith.

The Jesus Seminar is a group of New Testament scholars who, beginning in 1985, focused on the question "What did Jesus really say?" In answering this, the scholars examined all the ancient Christian documents with sig-

6. Much less using the term "son of Adam," a phrase that seems to have had little currency in the religious language of Palestinian Judaism (although it appears in Psalm 8:5 and Ezekiel 3:17).

nificant Jesus material, including canonical and extra-canonical texts like the *Gospel of Thomas*. *Thomas* is a collection of some one hundred and fifteen sayings of Jesus that undoubtedly predates the canonical gospels and was certainly used as one source by the New Testament writers for their "core" material. It was by no means the only text available in ancient Christian circles. In the first and early second centuries the number of gospels in circulation far outnumbered what came to be the canonical four, about a dozen of which we have in at least fragmentary form.[7]

Scholars take this material and attempt to arrange it in chronological layers, much as archaeologists try to strip away the chronological layers of a dig: Crusader period on top, Byzantine below, Roman below that, and so forth. Once the "dating" of a story or saying is made, then scholars look for as many independent occurrences, called "attestations," of the saying as they can. In other words, they ask, how many times do these words of Jesus occur in unrelated documents? This can be tricky, because not all attestations are necessarily independent. For example, if the saying appears in Mark, Matthew, and the *Gospel of Thomas*, that is probably two rather than three independent attestations because Matthew is likely to have picked up the saying from Mark. Obviously, the earlier the saying is, and the greater the number of independent attestations, the more likely it is that the story contains the words of the historical Jesus. Correspondingly, a single attestation found in a later stratum of material may well represent development or creation rather than retention.

---

7. Some of these gospels carry odd-sounding titles, such as *Dialogue of the Savior*, *Apocraphon of James*, and *Secret Mark*. The resource section provides information about these texts, now available in translation for readers interested in dipping into the extra-canonical literature.

Next, Bible scholars bring a whole host of methodologies from the literary and social sciences to bear on these passages, including cross-cultural anthropology, Hellenistic and Greco-Roman history, and what they can glean about the social world, religion, and politics of first-century Palestine, second-temple Judaism, and neighboring cultures. It is a very complex process of deciphering, and the process is far from reaching consensus, which is one of the reasons that there are now so many Jesus figures to consider.

The Jesus Seminar met twice a year for almost a decade to discuss and debate the more than fifteen hundred sayings of Jesus we have available, together with the data from other fields of research, and attempted to assess the authenticity of each saying according to a strict range of probabilities. Each member of the seminar then cast a "ballot" in the form of one of four colored beads: a red bead was a vote that "Jesus undoubtedly said this or something very like it"; a pink bead decided "Jesus probably said *something* like this"; a gray bead claimed "Jesus did not say this, but the ideas...are close to his own"; and a black one meant "Jesus did *not* say this; it represents...a later and/or different tradition." Only twenty percent of the sayings of Jesus came up either red or pink. So for those who grew up on the edition of the King James Bible in which every word attributed to Jesus is highlighted in red ink, including a huge chunk of the gospel of John, for example, this outcome is very disturbing. Many people also found the mere act of voting on the authenticity of the biblical texts not only arrogant but an affront to their most deeply held beliefs.

It is not surprising, then, that the historical Jesus project in general, and the Jesus Seminar in particular, have come under attack from evangelical Christians and scholars with a more orthodox understanding of the biblical Jesus.[8] Some of the criticisms, I think, are well founded. For example, the Jesus Seminar has probably been too restrictive; most of the material they regard as authentic are either aphorisms or parables, which effectively eliminates John's gospel from serious consideration since the Jesus of that gospel uses aphorisms sparingly and teaches no parables. My main quarrel with the historical Jesus project is that it tends to read the material for just two of its senses: the literal and the historical. As a largely academic effort, it tends to ignore the prophetic and spiritual senses of the Jesus literature—despite the fact that many who have engaged in this attempted work of "reconstruction" are themselves believers.

But what I find most odd about the debate is not the controversy generated—there is always controversy surrounding scholarship—but that some parties argue that the project is fundamentally misguided and ought to be abandoned. I think that is wrong. Indeed, when the modern search for the historical Jesus began in the 1950s, Ernst Käsemann, an eminent biblical scholar of the period, argued not only that the methods of New Testament studies were equal to the task, but that the task mattered, and it mattered most in terms of our understanding of discipleship.

If, for example, scholarly studies should demonstrate that Jesus was a Galilean peasant aligned with insurrectionist movements fighting the political hegemony of Roman colonialism and the religious elitism of second-temple Judaism, then it follows that contemporary disciples are called to fight against the social oppressions and religious

---

8. The seminar is currently attempting to determine what Jesus really *did*, moving its scrutiny from the sayings to the deeds. So the historical Jesus debates are not likely to go away any time soon.

aristocracies of our own day. Or should it emerge that the historical Jesus was primarily a peacemaker who espoused a politics of nonviolence and reconciliation, then the church in the public square today might emphasize that the work of peacemaking is not the exclusive domain of politicians. That view of Jesus is precisely what motivates the passivism of the Society of Friends and efforts such as the Christian Peace Initiative in Hebron.

In other words, the historical Jesus is at least one criterion for the church. He may not be the only, or even the ultimate, criterion, but if the believing community is meant to follow and not just to worship, it behooves us to take seriously the efforts to uncover, insofar as is possible, the vision and program of the Jesus of history.

～ So How Many Jesuses are There?

While the current furor makes it seem that Jesus has come under radical scrutiny for the first time, individuals and communities of faith have always tried to come to terms with their experience of him, and their efforts have produced some stunningly disparate images. In the same year that the Jesus Seminar began its work, Jaroslav Pelikan's *Jesus Through the Centuries*[9] argued that different dimensions of the Jesus of the Bible have emerged and receded with shifting cultural history. Pelikan notes, for example, that Jesus was the Rabbi in the first century, when Christianity and rabbinic Judaism were both developing; the King of Kings in the fourth- and fifth-century Roman Empire; the Monk Who Rules the World in the monastic culture of the Middle Ages; the Universal Man in the Renaissance; the

---

9. The book was reissued by Yale University Press in 1997, now lushly illustrated.

Teacher of Common Sense in the "enlightened" eighteenth century; and the Liberator in our own.

These images are just a sampling from history's sketchbook, and the contemporary historical Jesus project has at least as many sketches to add. Depending on what you read, the Jesus of current scholarship is an eschatological prophet, an itinerant Cynic sage, a social revolutionary, a teacher of an unconventional wisdom, a founder of a religious movement, or a shaman—that is, a mystical holy man. You can get a sense of this broad sweep from Marcus Borg, the biblical scholar who was once asked to summarize the pre-Easter Jesus for NBC's "Today Show" in a one-minute-fifteen-second sound bite.

> He was a peasant, which tells us about his social class. Clearly, he was brilliant. His use of language was remarkable and poetic, filled with images and stories. He had a metaphoric mind.
>
> He was not an ascetic, but world-affirming, with a zest for life. There was a sociopolitical passion to him. Like a Gandhi or a Martin Luther King, he challenged the domination system of his day.
>
> He was a religious ecstatic, a Jewish mystic...for whom God was an experiential reality. As such, he was also a healer. And there seems to have been a spiritual presence around him, like that reported of St. Francis or the Dalai Lama.
>
> And I suggest that as a figure of history, he was an ambiguous figure. You could experience him and conclude he was insane, as his family did [Mark 3:21]; or that he was simply eccentric; or that he was a dangerous threat; or you could conclude that he was filled with the spirit of God.[10]

As I have already suggested, if you want a set of complicated and ambiguous portraits of Jesus, there is no better place to find them than in the canonical gospels. The epistles of Paul—the apostle who never encountered the Jesus of history but only the Christ of faith (Acts 9:3-9; 1 Corinthians 15:8)—present another set of canvases altogether. In other words, the "Jesus problem" begins right on the pages of the New Testament. And what I would like to do in the remainder of this chapter is explore the Jesus of those pages, so that he might become more richly available to the community of faith.

～ The Jesus of the Passions

We could wander our way through the New Testament, teasing out the various Jesuses of its pages, but nowhere is this more easily—and perhaps more coherently—done than by examining the passion narratives, the stories of Jesus' suffering and death on the cross. These stories were almost surely the first written. In fact, I usually explain to Bible students that the gospels were written *backward* from the passion. When the earliest communities began to recite their memories of Jesus, and to wrestle with the meaning of their experiences of him, they began first with his suffering and death. That project eventually gave us the passion narratives, and these, in turn, shaped the character and significance of Jesus when the stories of his life and ministry began to be told and written later. In other words, four distinctly different passion accounts resulted in four different gospel stories of Jesus.

10.Marcus Borg, in a lecture given at the 27th National Conference of Trinity Institute, February 9, 1996.

Matthew

We will start with a single text from Matthew, chapter 5 verses 17 through 20. After reading it I think you can begin to appreciate how the author's understanding of the death came to shape his understanding of the life.

This passage—especially when you pay attention to its historical sense—reflects a particularly Matthean concern: he wants to establish unequivocally the Jewishness of Jesus. In fact, most scholars consider Matthew's gospel to be the most "Jewish" of the four. He is the only evangelist, for example, who opens his Jesus narrative with a detailed genealogy that traces the lineage of the Christ back to Abraham and stresses the Jewish interest in numerology:

> So all the generations from Abraham to David were fourteen generations; and from David to the deportation to Babylon, fourteen generations; and from the deportation to Babylon to the Messiah, fourteen generations. (Matthew 1:17)

Thus Matthew 5:17-20 gives us a text from Jesus' ministry in which Jesus endorses the law and stands in continuity with it. Luke's gospel makes a passing comment on the durability of the law—"It is easier for heaven and earth to pass away, than for one stroke of a letter in the law to be dropped" (16:17)—but Matthew is the evangelist most concerned with securing a place for Jesus within law and prophecy, and he understands the trial and crucifixion in terms of messianic prophecy fulfilled. Consider, for example, the incident at the arrest when one of Jesus' followers cuts off the ear of the high priest's slave:

> Then Jesus said to him, "Put your sword back into its place; for all who take the sword will perish by the sword. Do you think that I cannot appeal to my Father,

and he will at once send me more than twelve legions of angels? *But how then would the scriptures be fulfilled, which say it must happen in this way?* (Matthew 26:52–54, emphasis added)

It is not surprising, then, that when Jesus comes to teach on the law he defends it more emphatically in Matthew than in any other gospel; even his followers are to be more zealous for the law than some of its more elite custodians. That is the allusion he is making in 5:20: "Unless your righteousness exceeds that of the scribes and Pharisees, you will never enter the kingdom of heaven." In other words, the meaning of Jesus' death created the character of his life. For Matthew, Jesus is not so much an autonomous actor on an isolated and independent stage, but an agent of God's plan for all time, which is inexorably unfolding as the promise of all Jewish history. But that unfolding is seen in narrative retrospect from Matthew's theological vantage on the passion. Chapter 26, if you will, writes chapter 5.

A second example helps to make the point. All four of the gospels locate the arrest of Jesus on the Mount of Olives. And while only Matthew and Mark specify Gethsemane and John speaks generically of a "garden" across the Kidron Valley, the convergence of narrative geography suggests an historical basis in the tradition memory for this site. But Matthew makes special use of the location to link Jesus with the heroic King David. As recorded in 2 Samuel 15:30-31, David flees Jerusalem in peril of his life following Absalom's revolt; he goes to the Mount of Olives and weeps there, discovering that his most trusted friend and advisor, Ahithophel, has betrayed him. So it is perhaps no literary accident that Matthew uses the Mount of Olives to highlight the desertion of Jesus by his followers and the treachery of Judas.[11] The story of the Davidic messiah is meant to reach backward to the story of David, as Matthew makes clear in his account of the betrayal of Jesus by Judas (26:45-50, 55-56).

For Matthew, "all this has taken place, *so that the scriptures of the prophets may be fulfilled*" (26:56, emphasis added). Matthew's view of Jesus as the new and enfleshed Torah carries all the way through to the very end of the gospel:

> Go therefore and make disciples of all nations, baptizing them in the name of the Father and of the Son and of the Holy Spirit, and *teaching them to obey everything that I have commanded you.* And remember, I am with you always, to the end of the age. (Matthew 28:19-20, emphasis added)

Focus on that italicized phrase about teaching, and what you have here is a rabbinic Jesus who does not wish to scuttle the Mosaic law but has demonstrated its true observance in his life and ministry.

When you read Matthew for its literal and historical senses, the Jesus who emerges is the very flowering of the wisdom and spirit intrinsic to the epic of Israel. Written fifteen or twenty years after the destruction of the Temple—and when Torah was coming into prominence as the singular remnant of Judaism—the gospel of Matthew is a

---

11. Luke, by contrast, speaks very little about the failure of discipleship in his passion narrative, and he seems to connect Olivet with its second reference in the Hebrew Bible. In Zechariah 14:4ff, it is the site to which God will come on the day of judgment—a reference that accounts for why Luke names the mountain as the site of Jesus' ascension into heaven and the place of his ultimate return (Acts 1:9-12).

kind of handbook of instruction for a Jesus movement of largely Jewish identity that is trying to make peace with its Jewish neighbors. When you read it prophetically, especially with the Great Commission in mind, the Jesus of the Matthean community calls on his followers to carry his new Torah forward into all time.

Luke

In Luke's gospel, the suffering and the dying are vehicles for the healing and reconciling power of Jesus now revealed to the entire world. Take, for example, the exchange from the cross between Jesus and the pair of thieves crucified with him found in Luke 23:39-43. Only in Luke is there a "good thief" who is repentant on the cross and thereby promised a place in paradise.

Only in Luke does Jesus console the women of Jerusalem as he walks his way toward Golgotha. Only in Luke, nailed to the cross, does he pardon his executioners: "Father, forgive them; for they do not know what they are doing" (23:34). And only in Luke does the passion itself effect rapprochement between adversaries. In the Lucan trial, Jesus is shuffled back and forth between Pilate, the governor of Judea, and Herod Antipas, the tetrarch of Galilee, neither wanting to take responsibility for the sentencing and both wanting to claim that Jesus belongs to the other's jurisdiction. Nonetheless, "that same day Herod and Pilate became friends with each other; before this they had been enemies" (23:12). Given this, it is not at all surprising that the Jesus of Luke's ministry shows tenderness to a gentile widow of Nain (7:11-17), commends to his followers the behavior of a "good" Samaritan (10:29-37), and praises a father's lavish welcoming of his prodigal son (15:11-32). These three stories are found only in Luke, and they are narratives of a ministry that are congruent with Luke's understanding of the passion.

This congruence extends also to the relationship of Jesus with his followers and closest disciples: he treats them with extraordinary delicacy during his ministry, unlike Matthew who alludes to (and Mark who dwells on) their aggravating failures. And in the passion, Luke never mentions that they flee. In fact, their faithfulness to Jesus is underscored by his words at the Last Supper: "You are those who have stood by me in my trials; and I confer on you, just as my Father has conferred on me, a kingdom, so that you may eat and drink at my table in my kingdom" (22:28-30). Accordingly, in the garden, Jesus is not separated from the body of the twelve, as he is in Matthew, for solitary prayer. He simply withdraws from them "about a stone's throw" (22:41). If they sleep rather than pray with him—and he only finds them sleeping once, not three times—it is "because of grief" (22:45) and not because "the flesh is weak" (Matthew 26:41). Luke also adds a healing motif to the arrest scene which is unique to his narrative:

> And when those who were about him saw what was coming, they asked, "Lord, should we strike with the sword?" Then one of them struck the slave of the high priest and cut off his right ear. But Jesus said, "No more of this!" And he touched his ear and healed him. (Luke 22:49-51)

This Jesus, who so often healed in his ministry, now at the end of his life, heals even his opponents.

The Jesus of Luke's passion also serves as a model for the life and ministry he expects of the church. Accused by the chief priests before a Roman governor and a Herodian king, the apostle Paul is brought before the same cast of characters in the Book of Acts, which was also written by

Luke. It is interesting to read in Acts 21:27 through 25:27, where you will see how Luke's "passion narrative" for Paul runs along the same lines as those he constructs for Jesus. Likewise, if Jesus dies asking forgiveness for his enemies and commending his soul to God, the first Christian martyr—Stephen, stoned in Jerusalem—dies with roughly the same words on his lips:

> While they were stoning Stephen, he prayed, "Lord Jesus, receive my spirit." Then he knelt down and cried out in a loud voice, "Lord, do not hold this sin against them." And when he had said this, he died. (Acts 7:59-60)

In short, Luke's gospel not only reads backward from the passion to create an ever-reconciling, uniting, and healing Jesus, but it also reads *forward*—prophetically, if you will—through the evangelist's "second gospel" in Acts to a create a reconciling and healing discipleship for the church.

Mark and John

Nowhere, however, are the figures of Jesus more sharply contrasted than in the passion narratives of Mark (14:26–15:47) and John (18:1–19:42). Consider, for example, the dramatically different ways that Mark and John handle the issue of Jesus' acceptance of his ultimate fate. In the garden of Mark's story, the weight of the "cup" is so heavy that Jesus stumbles to the ground and pleads that

> if it were possible, the hour might pass from him. He said, "Abba, Father, for you all things are possible; remove this cup from me; yet, not what I want, but what you want." (Mark 14:35-36)

That last half-verse is a pledge of obedience, of course, but it is an anguished pledge indeed. In John, however, Jesus seems almost to relish his self-offering on the cross:

> Now is my soul troubled. And what should I say—"Father, save me from this hour?" No, it is for this reason that I have come to this hour. Father, glorify your name. (John 12:27-28)

In Mark, the passion story is dominated by the themes of abandonment and failure, and the failure is reversed by the in-breaking power of God only at the end of the drama (15:38-39). Mark asserts repeatedly that gain is achieved only through loss, that vindication comes only after humiliation, that resurrection follows only after crucifixion. The central moral of the story is *pascha et transitus:* new life results from passage through death.

Mark hints at abandonment early in Jesus' ministry by references to the failure of the twelve to comprehend the meaning of discipleship (8:31-33; 9:9-13, 31-32; 10:17-22, 35-38). These references crystallize in Jesus' prediction that his disciples' faithfulness will not endure his final trial: "You will all become deserters" (14:27). And indeed, they do: "All of them deserted him and fled" (14:50). From Gethsemane to Golgotha, the Jesus of Mark's gospel is increasingly isolated and alone. He moves with the twelve from their last meal together to the garden; there he separates himself, together with Peter, James, and John, from the larger body of his disciples (14:33); then he leaves behind even the inner circle to pray alone (14:35). The failure of the three to watch and pray with him anticipates the course that the rest of the narrative will run. No support will come from those who were his erstwhile friends. He will die alone, with only a small collection of women "looking on from a distance" (15:40).

In his book *A Christ Crucified in Holy Week*, biblical scholar Raymond Brown notes that at the baptism (Mark 1:11) and the transfiguration (Mark 9:7), Jesus was supported by a heavenly voice that affirmed his election as Son, but in his final trial the heavenly voice is silent. Alone in his agony, deserted by his followers, betrayed by Peter, scourged by Pilate's flunkies, ridiculed by the passersby, reviled by his executioners, the Markan Jesus will appear to be abandoned even by his *Abba*: from the cross he cries out, "My God, my God, why have you forsaken me?" (15:34). Only at the moment of death does the Father break into the narrative, and then only in the symbol of a torn curtain in the Temple and in the words of a Roman centurion: "Truly this man was God's Son!" (15:39).

The Jesus of John's passion, however, is very much in control of his trial, crucifixion, and death. He moves through the events of the passion with serenity and command. For example, consider now how John describes the arrest of Jesus in chapter 18, verses 3 through 11.

This Jesus, who knows "all that was to happen to him" (18:4) and who is willing to "drink the cup that the Father has given" him (18:11), is fully aware of his co-eternality with God, and so he knows that in dying he is simply returning to a reality temporarily vacated for his brief stay in the world (17:5). Moreover, he explains to his disciples that his departure assures a place for them in the Father's house of many rooms (14:2-3), insisting that unless he goes away the sustaining presence of the Holy Spirit will not come to them (14:16; 16:7). In the garden, he does not pray to be delivered from his agonies, but rephrases the Markan petition as a rhetorical question that demands a negative response: "And what should I say—'Father, save me from this hour?' No, it is for this reason that I have come to this hour" (12:27b).

Similarly, the Johannine Jesus is not a victim. He has freely chosen to lay down his life; no one takes it from him and he has the power to take it up again whenever he chooses (10:17-18). Nor is he at the mercy of his enemies: he has conquered the world even before his trial begins (16:33), and the cross only testifies to his victory. That victory is evidenced in many places in the narrative. Note, for example, that at the moment of the arrest, Jesus does not fall to the ground in despair as he does in Mark; instead, it is the Roman soldiers and the Jewish police who stumble in the dirt (18:4-6).

Finally, the Jesus of John's passion does not die alone. He is attended on Calvary by his mother and the disciple whom he loved, and this Jesus has no need to cry out to a God who has abandoned him to his suffering because God is always with him: "The Father and I are one" (10:30). In fact, Jesus' final words from the cross are not an anguished question (Mark's "Why have you deserted me?") but a solemn, decisive statement ("It is finished"). Only when *he* has decided that the work given to him by the Father is completed does he "hand over his spirit" (19:30)—a turn of phrase that also sets John's Jesus apart.[12]

In Mark, Jesus "breathes his last"; in Matthew, he "surrenders his spirit"; and in Luke, he "commends his spirit" to the Father. In each of these cases, the death is surrounded by a sense of passive release occasioned by forces beyond the influence of the crucified Lord. But in John, Jesus takes active control of his dying: he "hands over" his spirit. This phrase is not an accidental choice of words. The

---

12. Here is a case where the NRSV, which renders John's account "gave up his spirit," muddies the waters by inattention to the nuance of the Greek. John's verb is better translated as the more active "handing over," and not as a surrender of spirit.

Greek verb is *paradidomi* and in John there is an almost formulaic repetition of its use: Jesus is first "handed over" by the Jews to Pilate and then by Pilate for crucifixion, and finally Jesus "hands over" his spirit to those who stand at the foot of his cross, Mary and John. It is not, however, a surrender but the concluding piece of his mission in the world. And, if we read it prophetically, when Jesus "handed over" his spirit to his mother and his best-loved disciple, he created the family of believers who stood then, and stand even now, as witnesses to his ongoing presence and power. The key to understanding John's version of the passion is that crucifixion itself is glorification: *pascha et passio*, Easter and Good Friday are almost identical in John's mind.

It is fascinating to think for a moment about the two experiences of Jesus that stand behind these remarkably different accounts of the passion. It must have felt to Mark's community that their time with Jesus on the road to Calvary was like moving inexorably toward the death of hope, a future irretrievably lost. Thinking themselves abandoned, they scattered—only later to see that God had surprisingly effected an apocalyptic reversal of fortune. For John's people, it was just the opposite. As Jesus moved closer and closer to death, his glory shone with ever-increasing brilliance, and in that movement he mapped the path of glory for them as well: there is no greater love than to lay down one's life for one's friends.

Throughout the centuries the church has invited believing communities to share both experiences of Jesus through the liturgy. The Great Vigil of Easter is Markan; its shape is *pascha et transitus*. It begins in the darkness of the tomb of Good Friday, where a small, new fire is kindled. It includes the singing of an ancient hymn, the Exsultet, which bids God break in on the darkness of our death, ripping in shreds the veil of our isolation. And it moves from there to the first eucharist of Easter—lights full on, bells that have been silent all through Lent ringing loudly, often accompanied by trumpets and timpani. Victory emerges from apparent defeat.

The liturgy of Good Friday, however, is pure John. Since ancient times, and in the American prayer book today, the liturgy includes a number of hymns that extol the glory of the cross. One of these, the *Pange lingue*, speaks of "the triumph of the victim," reigning from the cross as king. That hymn derives from the sovereign Jesus of John's passion. Good Friday is the only day in the liturgical year when we physically venerate the cross. This is done not because we remember it as an instrument of death but as a platform of life from which its occupant's regal stature was announced in three languages. The Jesus of this passion has conquered the dominant powers of his world: Greek culture, Hebrew religion, and Roman law. It is significant that Pilate's trilingual inscription in the John narrative is hung not over the door of a tomb but above the royal head presiding from the Tree of Life.

If by some accident of history all of the gospel texts had been lost except John's, Good Friday—not Easter Day—would be our principal feast of the resurrection. But of course we do have all four gospels, each with its richly nuanced account of Jesus constructed from the earliest communities' differing memories and disparate experiences of his dying. None of the four, however, is definitive; we are invited into them all.

〜 But Who Do You Say That I Am?
In a profound sense, the Jesus who is assembled by the New Testament texts—forward and backward from the

passion narratives—is an invitation to ponder what our own lives and worlds could be like if we patterned them off his. And perhaps the most provocative invitation is given by the question Jesus posed to his disciples about himself.

> Jesus went on with his disciples to the villages of Cae-
> sarea Philippi; and on the way he asked his disciples,
> "Who do people say that I am?" And they answered
> him, "John the Baptist; and others, Elijah; and still oth-
> ers, one of the prophets." He asked them, "But who do
> you say that I am?" Peter answered him, "You are the
> Messiah." (Mark 8:27-30)

Peter's confession is almost assuredly the voice of the post-Easter community, reflecting on what Jesus had come to mean for their own lives and worlds. Still, some of its members must have had certain misapprehensions about what exactly it meant to be "the Christ," because the Jesus of this story later finds it necessary to correct Peter's messianic expectations: "Get behind me, Satan! For you are setting your mind not on divine but on human things" (8:33).

In the Matthean version (see Matthew 16:13-19), how-ever, Peter is not immediately rebuked (that comes later) but praised. The confession in Matthew's text takes a much more exalted view of Jesus than in Mark's. Like Mark, the narrative moves right ahead to the first predic-tion of the passion, but passion or not, it is a very high christology: "Blessed are you, Simon son of Jonah! For flesh and blood has not revealed this to you, but my Father in heaven" (16:17). When you think about it, the power and privilege entrusted in these lines to Simon son of Jo-nah says much more about the divinity of Jesus than it does about the primacy of Peter. This is a Jesus who is able to pass on the keys of the kingdom because they are his to give away.

I highlight the differences between these two versions to underscore what by now should be obvious: just as there is no simple and coherent theology of the God of the Bible, there is no simple and coherent christology of the Jesus of the New Testament. The Jesus of the Bible will not sit still for a single definitive portrait. He will not be boxed in.

Thus, we are left at the end of this chapter with the question I posed at the beginning still unanswered: "Who is the Jesus portrayed in the Bible?" But perhaps that is not the most urgent question; it is really only another way to ask, "Who do people say that I am?" That question seems peripheral, especially if we focus only on the literal and historical Jesus. But when we attend to the prophetic Jesus as well, what is primary and crucial is not the Jesus of record but the Jesus of experience and promise. He is ultimately assembled out of the lives and hopes of believing communities and faithful individuals. Who do *you* say that he is?

For some of us, he may be the teacher of an alternative wisdom who helps us rethink our place in this world; for others, he may be the power of a Twelve-Step resurrection movement from the darkness of addiction to the light of recovery. For some, he may be a liberating release from whatever in life oppresses; for still others, he may be the pivot point of prayer who tips toward the presence of God. All of these are inclusive of the Jesus of history *and* the Christ of faith, and none is exhaustive.

When we give him all the space he needs to enter our own realities, Jesus becomes not just our past but our present and our future as well. Mark says as much in the concluding verses of his gospel: "He is not here. Look, there is the place they laid him. But go, tell his disciples and Peter that he is going ahead of you to Galilee; there you will see him, just as he told you" (16:6-7). In the end, Jesus is never just behind us, either in text or tradition. He is always out in front, leading us toward some new adventure of himself—and of ourselves in him. The angel at the empty tomb in Luke (24:5) puts it this way: "Why do you look for the living among the dead?"

~ Chapter 8

The Word as Sacrament

Peter Gomes, Baptist minister at Harvard University's Memorial Church and author of *The Good Book: Reading the Bible with Mind and Heart*, points out that "the Episcopal Church, while not known as a *Bible* church in the sense of those evangelical and free churches that advertise themselves as such, nevertheless exposes its worshipers to a great deal of scripture on Sunday mornings."[1] But this was not always so. When I was growing up in the Episcopal Church of the fifties and sixties, the Bible was not in any way extensively read as part of regular worship. The Sunday eucharistic lectionary of the 1928 *Book of Common Prayer* called only for a reading from one of the epistles and one of the gospels, and the same cycle of readings repeated itself on a yearly basis. So if you were a member of an Anglo-Catholic parish, as I was, where "attending mass" was the *essential* act of piety, you never heard a sentence of the Hebrew Bible uttered in church. That was left to the monks and nuns of our monastic communities as they re-

---

1. Peter Gomes, *The Good Book: Reading the Bible with Mind and Heart* (New York: William Morrow & Co., 1996), 10.

cited their "daily offices." On the other hand, the "Morning Prayer parishes," like their monastic brothers and sisters, read lessons from both the Old *and* the New Testaments; so at least they heard something of the Hebrew Bible. But that aspect of worship did not seem nearly as important as the mass to us, and we deplored the practice of relegating the service of Holy Communion to some isolated early hour, like 7 A.M.! We "high church" folk snobbishly considered "Morning Prayer Episcopalians" as irredeemably "Protestant." And it never occurred to us that there was a biblical richness available in Morning and Evening Prayer that was missing from eucharistic worship because of the absence of the Old Testament texts.

All of that changed—including the mutually dismissive bickering between "high church" and "low church" factions—with the introduction of the 1979 edition of the *Book of Common Prayer.* With the arrival of the new prayer book, which, of course, is by now not *new* at all, came the enormously expanded contact with Holy Scripture to which Peter Gomes refers. Now the eucharistic lectionary appoints three readings plus a psalm selection for every Sunday: a gospel and an epistle, as before, but also a mandatory reading from the Hebrew Bible. And the cycle repeats itself only every third year. Year A focuses on the gospel of Matthew, Year B on Mark, and Year C on Luke, with ample selections from John added into each of the three years, particularly during special seasons such as Christmas, Holy Week, and Eastertide. Likewise, the readings appointed for the daily offices of Morning and Evening Prayer are much expanded and repeated over a two-year reading cycle. In fact, if you attended each of these services on a daily basis, you would hear almost the entire Bible during that two-year period. And all one hundred fifty psalms during a single month!

That is indeed a great deal of contact with the Bible in worship, and part of the motivation has come from a church trying to respond to the voices of its laity, who were the first to demand increased biblical literacy. But I also think that over the last generation—and this is reflected in our newer emphasis on the Bible in worship—we have become a church that understands that the Word provides as much access to divine presence as the bread and wine of the eucharist. In other words, Scripture has become more *sacramental* for us than it used to be. What I would like to do in this chapter is explore what it means for *word* to be *sacrament*, for *story* to be as spiritually important as *table*. But let me begin with an anecdote that is fundamentally rooted in our Hebraic past.

∾ Laying *Tefilin*: The Word in Hebrew Prayer

In midsummer 1994, I found myself on a flight to Tel Aviv with about a hundred teenagers from a number of Hebrew schools in Mexico. They had been in New York City for the World Cup games and were on their way to be farmed out for a month in a dozen different *kibbutzim* in Israel. They were lovely kids, full of excitement and the sense of adventure that comes from traveling without your parents when you are young.

El Al Flight 17 took off around midnight, and by the time we had been given the slow service that kills time over the Atlantic drinks, dinner, duty-free sales, and movies—it began to be dawn outside. That is when the Jewish boys began to pray. The Jewish men slept. They prayed by the clock, not the sun, mustering a more or less wakeful *minyan*—the ten required for official synagogue worship—in the back of the plane. But the kids prayed singly, starting at first light, and since there was a lot of first light as we crossed the Atlantic, then the northern half of Europe, and finally the eastern Adriatic, somewhere on the airplane there was almost always a boy wrapped in his prayer shawl, bobbing in the aisles, and muttering what I suspect was Spanish-accented Hebrew.

Perhaps Leviticus stipulates that you cannot pray with a foreign object in your mouth, and a fair number of the kids wore retainers. So prayer began with the boy taking his retainer out and putting it in a little case. Then out of another little case came the phylacteries, the small box with its attached leather bands that is worn by an Orthodox Jew when he prays. The boy would secure the box to his forehead and then wind its thongs around his left arm. Then the prayer shawl, wrapped around his shoulders; then the prayer book opened; then the prayers recited. At the end of his prayers the ritual was reversed. The shawl was put away in its beautifully embroidered silk pouch; the phylacteries were unwound, removed, and stowed; and the retainer was put back in the mouth. It was wonderful to watch a boy transformed into a *bar mitzvahed*, that is, an adult, pray-er, and then see him transformed back into a teenager who is probably more at home with tennis than Torah, his teeth not yet straight.

The rite of praying with the phylacteries is called "to lay *tefilin*," and every Orthodox Jewish male lays *tefilin* every day. But what is the little box about, and the thongs? Why this ceremonial? What is going on in this ritual? To answer these questions, we need to look at a transformation we can see happening in the Hebrew Bible itself.

The oldest parts of the scriptures, the five books of Moses, contain the stories of the birth of a nation. Among these stories, and often inseparable from them, are the laws that gave original shape to that nation's people—the Decalogue, or the Ten Commandments, of course, but all of the Levitical and Deuteronomic codes as well. Taken together, the histories and the laws in these five books constitute Torah. At one level, you can think about Torah as a set of organizing principles that assemble a sacred people: it outlines their identity, the terms of their relationship with their God, and their modes of behavior with one another.

As religious thought developed within the Hebraic tradition, however, particularly in the prophetic tradition, the law once written on stone tablets was meant to be written in the heart. Torah began both to organize the outward life of the community and the inward life of the individual Jew. You can think about the move from the one to the other as a shift from an exterior formula for how to be *with* God to an interior reality of God's being *within*. I do not mean to suggest that the view of Torah evolved so that the private spirituality of the individual Jew came to displace his public responsibility. Engagement with both was, and is, incumbent on the believer, and the two have long been inextricably linked. In fact, when Torah is written in the heart, it follows that it will flow outward to shape one's every engagement with community and world.

Laying *tefilin* is a ritual symbolizing this movement from exterior piety to interior presence. The little box affixed to the forehead contains a piece of Torah, a bit of scroll, a portion of the law. It is placed on the brow so that Torah might occupy your mind. And the left arm, wrapped with the bands of the phylacteries, is the arm closer to your heart when you hold the prayer book in your hands and bob in rhythm with its words. The symbolism of the ritual is clear: to lay *tefilin*, to bring the Word of God into direct bodily contact, is to pray that God will choose to dwell within you.

We have something of this ritual in Christian worship too. At the reading of the gospel in the eucharist, the deacon or priest makes a small sign of the cross on the first word of the text appointed for the day and then repeats the sign three times: on the forehead, on the lips, and on the breast—just over the heart. In response to the announcement, the congregation imitates the three signs. This small ritual observance, like laying *tefilin*, is itself a prayer that the Word of God will take up residence within. As a child, I was taught just such a prayer to recite while making the signs: that God would be in my mind, on my lips, and in my heart. When the deacon who is reading the gospel moves her thumb from signing the book to signing her brow, she is—on behalf of all the worshiping community—moving the Word from the page of the book to those parts of our bodies that think, speak, and love, from exterior formula to interior reality. And it follows that when the gospel, like Torah, takes up residence in our hearts, it will flow outward from there to shape our involvement with community and world. These liturgical gestures are icons of the life of Holy Scripture in the life of the community at worship.

∾ Moving the Texts Inside: Eucharistic Praying

William Palmer Ladd, a much revered dean of the Berkeley Divinity School early in this century, was reportedly fond of saying that the *Book of Common Prayer* takes the Bible and makes liturgy out of it. This use of Scripture for shaping liturgy is not unique, however; long before Archbishop Thomas Cranmer fashioned the first Anglican worship book in 1549, Christian people were praying their texts. Nonetheless, Dean Ladd's remark underscores the timeless relationship between word and worship and the way in which prayer has arisen from story. Scripture functions in the liturgical life of the community in all the ways we have talked about in these pages. It tells the community who it has been; it creates an encounter between itself and the community's local place and present life; and it guides the community in imagining its future. But in worship especially, Scripture helps to create the sacred space in which the community comes to *be* in the presence of God. In other words, it becomes sacramental—a sign of God's reality among us. For eucharistic worshipers there are two focal signs of God's presence in the liturgy: Word spoken and Bread broken. This has been so from the start.

The earliest Christians encountered the presence of God first as Word spoken and Teaching heard, a kind of Torah but with new meaning in the person of Jesus of Nazareth. After his death and resurrection, when this powerful new reality lived on both in the memorial meal they shared and in the stories of his life they told, something changed. The first followers began to talk about their experience of Jesus' life in terms of the *logos* of God made flesh, and they spoke of his death in terms of bread as body broken and wine as blood poured out. Those changes in language reflect movements of experience from exterior formula to interior presence. You can see them happening already in the pages of the New Testament, perhaps nowhere more clearly than in the bread of life discourse in John 6:25-59. Stop here for the moment and take time to read the passage; it is a long piece of text that is not easily summarized.

One of the unique features of John's gospel is that right after recording an event in the life of Jesus, the evangelist routinely provides an interpretation. Immediately before the text you have just read, the miracles—called "signs" by John—of the feeding of the five thousand and the walking on water have been recounted; those stories occupy the first twenty-one verses of chapter six. Now John devotes his concluding fifty verses to theological reflection on the meaning of the signs contained in the stories. The interpretive discourse opens in 6:25 with the crowd addressing Jesus specifically as "Rabbi." The title alone is your first clue that what follows (vv. 26-34) is going to present Jesus as a Jewish teacher. In fact, it is always a good idea to pay attention to the forms of address and titles for Jesus in the gospels; they are never used randomly. John then goes to some trouble to associate Jesus with Moses, the first teacher of Israel, who delivered Yahweh's law to the nation. In the Hebraic tradition, Moses is understood as a *tahib*, one who speaks for God; now Jesus assumes the mantle of the one who reveals what God wants spoken.

The crowd, however, wants to know whether Jesus is authorized to speak for God, and that is why they ask him, in verse 30, for a sign that his teaching is worth listening to. Not surprisingly, they refer to Moses' feeding their ancestors as just the sort of credible sign they are looking for: "He gave them bread from heaven to eat" (6:31). To which Jesus responds, "Listen, it wasn't Moses who gave the bread, it is my Father who gives the true bread!" This exchange is telling; it is cast in the shape of traditional Jewish teaching in which a passage from Scripture is cited and then the teacher shows that it has been incorrectly applied to the situation at hand—which is precisely what Jesus does here. He says, in effect, "Don't read the pronoun *he* as *Moses*; read it as *my Father.* And don't read the past tense of the verb, *gave*; read the present tense, *gives.* " The crowd, now satisfied that Jesus is skilled in the rabbinic methodology for exegesis, asks him to give *them* that true bread always.

That request raises two questions: what precisely is "true bread" and what is being taught? What is being taught is the wisdom of God, which is the "food that endures for eternal life." I make that assessment by noting especially the multiple uses of the word *work* and its plural in this section of the text. The work of God is so frequently associated with God's wisdom in the New Testament that *ergon* (work) and *sophia* (wisdom) are virtually interchangeable terms. Jesus' own work of feeding the multitude with the loaves is a sign that God's wisdom has come into the world for those who are hungry for it. This bread does not perish—not because it does not spoil, but because it has enduring substance. It feeds because it teaches God's truth, and learning that truth is to know eternal life.

The bread of life metaphor begins to take on added meaning, however, beginning with verse 35 and running through verse 47. Prompted by the crowd's request for the bread that lasts, Jesus responds, "I am the bread of life." That is a startling change. Jesus now equates *himself* with the wisdom of God: whoever comes to Jesus and his teachings will be taught by God's *sophia* (6:45). Less obvious, however, is the fact that we are dealing here with one of the several instances in John's gospel of the "I am" sayings (*ego eimi*, in the Greek): "I am the good shepherd" (10:11); "I am the true vine" (15:1); "I am the light of the world" (8:12); "I am the resurrection" (11:25). *Ego eimi* is the phrase Yahweh uses when Moses asks for God's name on Mount Sinai: "I am who I am" (Exodus 3:14, LXX).[2] Those Old Testament words are exactly what John wants his readers to hear when Jesus uses the phrase about himself. Thus, the self-referential "I am the bread of life" is a claim both highly nuanced and highly charged. Essentially, the equation reads:

---

2. The Septuagint (LXX) mistranslates the sentence into present tense. The Hebrew original is unambiguously future tense: "I will be who I will be."

Jesus = wisdom of God = God

We are not surprised, then, to learn in verse 41 that the Jews protest. Jesus is no longer claiming to be merely the teacher of God's wisdom; he is claiming to be that which is taught!

In the final section, verses 48 through 58, the bread of life image undergoes its third transformation. The evangelist gives you fair warning about this when, in verse 48, he has Jesus say for the second time, "I am the bread of life." This hardly needs repeating unless the phrase is going to take on new meaning. Here the meaning is now unmistakably eucharistic. The "bread of life" becomes symbolic of Jesus' body, and to experience eternal life, the believer must eat that bread. "Those who eat my flesh and drink my blood abide in me, and I in them" (6:56). That last phrase is the final movement in the text: abiding in him so that he may abide in us is the tangible, and yet timeless, point of contact between Jesus and his family of believers.

In his book entitled *The Mystical Way in the Fourth Gospel*, New Testament scholar William Countryman also talks about this discourse as a text of movement. It begins, he argues, as a story of enlightenment *about* God and ends as a story about union *with* God. Countryman adds that when you have moved in your own spiritual journey from knowing *about* Jesus to *knowing* Jesus' presence in your life, you have begun "to cross over into God."[3] That is what I mean by the sacramental character of Holy Scripture in worship. The Word begins as a way to enlighten the community about God and about itself; it ends by being

---

3. L. William Countryman, *The Mystical Way in the Fourth Gospel* (Philadelphia: Fortress Press, 1987).

the sacred place where the community crosses over into God.

～ Keeping the Way Clear: Preaching the Text

If Word and Table are the places where we cross over to God in the liturgy, then it follows that the community must have open access to the routes—and perhaps some road maps. But the way in must be kept clear. One of the worshiping community's routes to God through the Word is in hearing it preached. The pulpit is the place where the Word is broken open, just as the bread is broken open at the altar. So the sermon is a potential "God-place" for the community at prayer.

Preaching is fearsome. The problem for the preacher is often not so much having to render a strange story intelligible for modern hearers, but that the story itself renders a very strange God. You will recall from chapter 6 that the God of our stories provokes radical thinking, challenges conventional wisdom and behavior, and defies all reasonable human expectations of what God ought to be. That is very difficult to proclaim Sunday by Sunday, year in and year out. When much of our sacred literature looks like bad news for the world as we know it, a considerable burden is placed on the preacher—who has to have what I call a "paschal imagination." Often this imagination must work overtime to turn what looks like bad news into Good News. Preaching must draw the congregation to the edge of a direct and sustained encounter with the awful, wonderful, and transforming Word.

Walter Brueggemann, a preacher himself as well as a biblical scholar, talks about "a homiletical gap" that exists between the Word and those who hear it. It is not so much a gap of time and culture between the world of Jesus and our own, although that space does need to be crossed, nor is it merely a communication gap between the speaker and the listener. It is the distance between a transforming gospel and an untransformed community. When I have taught preaching, I have referred to this gap as the "combat zone." The Word is difficult and dangerous, a threat to complacency, so it is quite natural for the preacher to want to cushion the bumpy road.

Some of the cushions preachers use are liturgical. In some churches elaborate rituals surround the reading of Scripture—the book held high in procession, candles, sometimes incense, and the ceremonial veneration of the sacred page itself. But ritual can serve to place the experience of the Word at some distance, isolated from the lives of the listeners, venerated but not touched. Other "cushions" are rhetorical. I grew up in churches where almost every sermon began either with an attribution to the Holy Trinity ("In the name of...") or with a petition that the musings of the preacher be favorably regarded by the Deity ("Let the words of my mouth and the meditations of my heart be always acceptable..."). Almost every sermon ended either with a repetition of its opening Trinitarian allusion or, more often, with a sentence of doxology to the Trinity's first person: "And now unto God the Father be ascribed, as is most justly due, all Might, Majesty, Dominion, and Power." In the latter case, you could almost hear the capital letters in the tone of the preacher's voice. Devices like these disrupt the continuity between the Word spoken out and the Word broken open. Like the candles and incense around the reading of the gospel, they create a safe space around dangerous preaching where the congregation is more or less told to be at ease. They break—disassemble—the vital connection between the community and the texts that have assembled it. When that happens, the sermon does not allow us to "cross over" into God.

Crossing over occurs, I think, when the sermon is open-ended, not closed-off. One of the difficulties of preaching lies in its very nature: a sermon is the solitary crafting of a single pray er, more monologue than dialogue. Preachers will tell you that they preach as much to themselves as to their congregations, meaning that the sermon has emerged out of reflection on the things that the preacher needs to hear! The problem with that, of course, is that the homily can end up being a personal story, an offering to God from the heart of the preacher with the congregation just listening in.

For the Word of God to enliven, the preaching of it needs to be a community conversation, and the conversation needs to be ongoing. The evangelical tradition—especially the black evangelical tradition where the congregation is in actual dialogue with the preacher—is better at this than those of us in the Anglican tradition, although the "dialogue sermon" is not unknown in our churches. There are other ways to attack the problem, however. In one parish I served, we had a brown-bag lunch and Bible study after the Wednesday noon eucharist. The propers were always the texts for the upcoming Sunday, and we would have just used them as the readings for the midweek service as well. Then on Sunday mornings we had a group that discussed the texts and sermon from the previous Sunday, copies of which were available after it has been preached. The Wednesday group was clergy-led while the Sunday group was led by lay people; sometimes the preacher was there and sometimes not.

This pair of study groups served both as preface and postscript to the sermon preached that week, and they gave people in the parish an opportunity to gather up and reflect on some of its scattered pieces both before and after. They also gave the preacher an opportunity to listen more closely to the different "voices" that helped to shape the sermon—Scripture, surrounding culture, and particular community—and keep it from becoming a monologue instead of a conversation. So the conversation that took place around the sermon remained open-ended for about a ten-day period, and sometimes even longer, because the Word echoes.

❧ Moving the Texts Outside: Eucharistic Praxis

Let us assume that some measure of "crossing over" does happen in the life of the community at worship, and that the Word it has heard moves from just being an exterior principle to a profound sense of God's interior presence. What is next for the eucharistic community? Its encounter with God through word and sacrament moves it outward to a greater involvement with the world. Eucharistic prayer is followed by eucharistic *praxis*—a word meant to connote the fusion of prayer and action. Now written in the heart of a transformed, praying community, the Word must also be writ large in an untransformed, unbelieving world. It must be spoken and lived; transformation of the individual heart is only one side of the coin. The message of the gospels is not primarily about effecting a change in personal piety; the vision of the kingdom of God is grounded in a social program: "Cure the sick, raise the dead, cleanse the lepers, cast out demons" (Matthew 10:8). When the vision of Jesus comes to reside in the heart of the believing community, the community engages the social program—from the cobbled back alleys of London's East End slums to the corporate boardrooms of Chicago. The eucharist itself does not just memorialize Christ's sacrifice and death; it brings to life his vision for a transformed world.

I see this call to eucharistic praxis nowhere more dramatically than in the linked stories of the transfiguration and the healing of the epileptic boy told in Matthew, Mark, and Luke. In all three gospels, the stories are placed side by side. Once more, read at least the version of the pair found in Mark 9:2-8,14-29.[4]

The transfiguration is an apocalyptic incident in the story of Jesus, a moment when God dramatically breaks into the text. What we have in this story is a salvation history "summit conference" with Jesus, Moses, and Elijah gathered together on a hilltop. It would not have been lost on Mark's first hearers that Moses and Elijah are there to testify to Jesus; the voice from the cloud is not even needed. The narrative placement of Moses and Elijah—the two symbols of law and prophecy—on either side of Jesus tells us that the cross now stands with the law and the prophets and is affirmed by them.

In the passage, Peter not only adds his endorsement to this testimony, he suggests that a cult of adulation should form around it. "Master," he says, "it is a fine thing for us to be here. Let us make three tents—one for you, one for Moses, and one for Elijah." In effect, Peter wants to try to contain God's glory. He is proposing not only to camp out on this hill but to build safe houses for God, thereby avoiding the journey to Jerusalem for his Savior and his own eventual walk to Calvary.

The problem with tent-building is that one is not allowed to stay privately with the divine presence for very

---

4. You can skip the five verses that bridge the two incidents (9:9-13); these explain, essentially, that John the Baptist—now dead in the narrative chronology—was Elijah returned.

long. One is meant to come off the mountain of theophanic glory and walk the via crucis, the way of the cross. An epiphany is not an occasion for worship; it occurs in the midst of ordinary life so that ordinary life can be encouraged and empowered for discipleship. I think this movement—from worship to work—is the reason why the healing of the boy takes place right after the transfiguration. Jesus moves quickly to his next piece of healing business; he abdicates his throne to enter the throes of the world.

The Italian Renaissance painter Raphael understood the meaning of this when he painted these two stories together on a single canvas, a kind of horizontal diptych. In the upper half of his painting Jesus is suspended above the mountain of the transfiguration, wrapped in radiant white light and wearing an expression of beatific detachment. Below, at the base of the hill, everything is a swirl of color and chaos: the crowd; the apparently convulsing boy, mouth agape, eyes rolled back, twisted torso supported by an anguished father; the disciples, frantically gesturing—some in the direction of Jesus, perhaps indicating the source of a cure they have not been able to effect.

Art historians have puzzled over this work, wondering why Raphael juxtaposed a victory above and a defeat below. But the painting can be read another way: the boy in the painting could be at the end of his seizure. His wild eyes and his open mouth are consistent with the confusion *following* the spasmodic episode of an epileptic incident. Instead of depicting him in the midst of an attack, the artist shows the boy coming out of his convulsion: victory not over defeat, but victory over victory.[5] Raphael may have rendered him cured, which is what the presence and power of God working through Jesus always accomplishes. And if through Jesus, then also through us. Gospel and canvas agree on this point: discipleship is not the building of booths for worship, but the tending of the bruises of the world. Godly presence creates transforming power. Christian life is not about kneeling in reverence before the Blessed Sacrament enshrined in a tabernacle on an altar. We are meant to come down from our mountains of celestial vision, leaving behind whatever booths we have built in our moments of awe, to help transfigure *this* time and place.

5. This argument was suggested by Gordon Bendersky, a Philadelphia professor of medicine and an amateur art sleuth, in an article reported in *The New York Times* (December 16, 1995).

Finding Jesus

Exploring the geography of the land of the Bible today can be a very disconcerting adventure. So much of what you know from the biblical texts is found side by side in such a small space—with multiple sites for the most sacred events! There are, for example, two sites for Calvary only yards apart in the Church of the Holy Sepulchre in Jerusalem. Built over one is a Greek Orthodox altar; over the other, an Armenian shrine. Then there is the problem of Matthew's Sermon on the Mount and Luke's Sermon on the Plain. Were the Beatitudes preached on a hill above Capernaum or from a more level place just below? And did the transfiguration occur on Mount Hermon, which is on Israel's borders with Lebanon and Syria, at the tip of the northernmost finger of the Galilee, or on Mount Tabor, which is in the center of its palm?

In modern Jordan, I have visited two of at least three sites where Moses struck water from the rock. Similarly, back in the early part of this century, no one was sure exactly which of two adjacent locations on Mount Nebo was the place from which Moses surveyed the promised land, so the Franciscans secured rights to excavate them both. By contrast, the site where Jacob wrestled with the angel is clearly and conveniently located right alongside the main highway running north from Amman. All you need to do is ask your driver to pull onto the shoulder, scramble over a guardrail, slide down an embankment, and you are standing on holy ground.

If you do not bring a certain measure of detachment to your encounter with the land of the Bible, the experience can be rather surreal, like the religious equivalent of a visit to Disney World. Perhaps the most difficult of all is the pilgrim's first encounter with the Church of the Holy Sepulchre, and not only because of its two sites for Calvary. One expects this central shrine of Christendom to stand in isolated and majestic splendor, like St. Peter's in Rome or Notre Dame in Paris. But the anonymous buildings surrounding the Resurrection Church, as it is known in the East, cling to it like so many barnacles on the hull of a battered ship. If you come to it looking for numinous light, you find that it is dark and cramped. You hope for peace within its walls but instead are assailed by the chattering of tourists and the chants of clerics. You look for holiness but find jealousy: the six groups of occupants—Armenians, Copts, Ethiopians, Syrians, Latin Catholics, and Greek Orthodox—watch one another suspiciously for any infringement of territorial rights. Slightly overwhelmed by this church in particular, and the land of the Bible in general, one woman said to me bluntly, "Where do you expect us to find Jesus in all of this?"

The answer, of course, is that Jesus long ago moved outside space and time into eternity and faith. You can, however, find him in Emmaus. Not in the actual village—in fact, there are four villages that have claimed to be Emmaus at one time or another in the twenty centuries of Christian history. But you can find Jesus in the *experience* of Emmaus, which is described in Luke's account of the first Easter Day. Take up your Bible and read the story in Luke 24:13-35.

After you have finished reading, think about what this text says about the experience of Jesus' first followers. John Dominic Crossan argues that two groups of Christians emerged during the years immediately after the death of Jesus, in the first decades between the Jesus of history and the Christ of the gospels. One of these Crossan calls "mimetic," the other "exegetical." Mimetic Christians were the followers of Jesus who wandered around Palestine doing what he had done, imitating his ministry. They were probably illiterate peasants and itinerant proclaimers, announcing his ecstatic vision and practicing his social program. Moving from village to village, like the seventy sent out two by two, they traversed Judea, Samaria, and Galilee, offering free healing in exchange for open table fellowship. Crossan suspects that many of these folks might have gone for weeks without knowing about the events in Jerusalem. When they did learn that Jesus had been crucified, their response might have been something like this: "Well, that makes us sad. But he told us this would happen. And in any case, so long as we are out here teaching what he taught and doing what he did, the kingdom has arrived." This is the group of people with whom we might associate what biblical scholars have long called "the oral tradition," those who kept alive the sayings and teachings of Jesus and passed them on to others.

Back in Jerusalem, this theory goes, was a different group of Jesus' followers who were members of the literate class of teachers and scribes. There had been something so compelling about the Galilean rabbi that he had captured their hearts and minds even though they did not know quite what to make of him. I can easily imagine just that sort of attraction: entitled and educated North Ameri-

can Christians have been similarly captivated by their en-
counters with the poor and illiterate churches of Central
and South America, despite the class and cultural distance
between Salvador and San Francisco. In any case, after the
crucifixion these exegetical Christians were searching for
ways to understand the meaning of Jesus in their lives,
and they went to their sacred texts for answers.

Literate classes always tend to read and reflect before
they act, so the exegetical Christians, unlike their mimetic
counterparts, went not to the road but first to the book,
where they found in its pages the Suffering Servant of
Isaiah and the ritual notes for Yom Kippur, the Day of
Atonement. The atonement liturgy specifies that one of
two goats, a scapegoat bearing the sins of the nation on its
back, is to be sent out of the Temple precincts in Jerusalem
and into the desert to die. It is spat upon en route and prod-
ded along its way with reeds poked in its sides. The exegetical Christians would have read passages like these—and
hundreds of others—in light of their experience of Jesus
and exclaimed, "Of course! This is who he was." Their interpretive method is called "typological," and it is one of
the time-honored ways in which Christians have read the
Hebrew Bible. In fact, you see it used even in the New Testament. Whenever you run across the phrase "that the scriptures might be fulfilled," or some variation on it, you are
seeing on the page the fingerprints of the scribal Christians—who were first of all Jews, shaped by Torah.

Crossan draws his conclusions not from speculation
but from careful reading of the texts—all of them, not just
the authorized ones. But the strands of the mimetic and
exegetical traditions are wrapped around each other in the
canonical literature, as I think you can see very clearly in
the Emmaus story. The mimetic strand is obvious in the
itinerant theme: the followers are out there "on the road,"

doing what Jesus did, two by two. The tradition is also clear in their urging Jesus to share their evening meal; that is the theme of open table fellowship. But you can also see the exegetical strand at work when Jesus reveals to the pair of travelers the meanings of their sacred stories. There Jesus himself does exactly what the scribal Christians were doing: he explains his life and death in terms of the Hebrew Bible, "beginning with Moses and all the prophets" (24:27).

What I find most powerful about the Emmaus text, however, is that it explains to us where we can find Jesus. Strip away all but two of its twenty-two verses, and the places where we can find Jesus are clearly marked: in storytelling and in bread-breaking.

> Then beginning with Moses and all the prophets, he interpreted to them the things about himself in all the scriptures. (24:27)

> When he was at the table with them, he took bread, blessed and broke it, and gave it to them. Then their eyes were opened, and they recognized him. (24:30-31)

Think about these lines not as historical documentary or as narrative biography, leave aside even mimesis and exegesis, and what you have here is the location of the Risen One in the life of the believing community, then and now. Story and meal is where we find him. It is that simple. Meal and story are together at the center of Christian life, but it is the story that brings you to the table. So think of those stories, told over and over again, that never fail to cause a burning in your heart. What your heart recognizes is Jesus standing in the middle of your road. As the book of Deuteronomy said first, "The Word is very near you."

Resources

Bible reading is an investment that requires considerable time and energy. It is hard work, and at the outset, you will need some assistance. But becoming an adept at reading the Bible is not an impossible task, and in what follows I offer some aids for making the task less intimidating, both for individuals reading alone and communities reading together.

∾ Translations
Since the average parish reading group is unlikely to include a linguist trained in Hebrew and Greek, consult as many different translations of a text as you can lay your hands on. These will give you a sense of the range of decisions that translators have had to make when bringing the ancient texts into current idiom. In fact, there is no final authoritative word, no autographed original, that provides an undisputed reading of a biblical text. Even the New Testament in Greek is the product of hundreds of editorial decisions, compiled from comparisons of multiple copies of ancient manuscripts, most of them fragmentary.

Translations fall roughly into one of two types: the first is called a "formal equivalent" translation; the second, a "dynamic equivalent" translation. The former attempts to achieve a more or less literal correspondence between the original language and the translated version, with just enough play so as to avoid stilted construction and awkward phrasings in English. The latter is less concerned with literal correspondence and runs in the direction of paraphrase. On the whole, the formal equivalent translation will be a more reliable rendering of the ancient languages, and the *Revised Standard Version* achieves this, as does the *New English Bible* and the *Jerusalem Bible*. The *New Revised Standard Version* (NRSV) also claims formal equivalency but, in my opinion, does not achieve it quite as successfully as the earlier version.

The NRSV, however, has rapidly become the "church's book," widely used now for the readings at the Sunday eucharists in Episcopal parishes. And that may be a very good reason *not* to use it in your Bible study; familiarity over time with a single text tends to give it too much authority. The very popular *Good News Bible* is a decidedly dynamic equivalent translation. I do not recommend it for routine study, nor its close relative *The Living Bible*, which is an obvious paraphrase. These need to be read with caution because they often contain theological agendas masquerading as translations. *The Living Bible*, for example, regularly translates the Pauline word "righteousness" with the phrase "getting right with God"—which does considerable violence not only to Paul's coinage but also to his theology.

Several intriguing new translations of portions of the Bible are now available. Among the freshest of these is Everett Fox's *Five Books of Moses* (Schocken, 1995), offering an English rendering of the Pentateuch that attempts to echo the sound structure and cadence of the oral Hebrew. Richard Lattimore, well known for his translations of the Homeric literature, has now collected his New Testament translations into a single volume called *The New Testament* (North Point Press/Farrar, Strauss, Giroux, 1996). One very good attempt at a gender-neutral translation is *The Inclusive New Testament* (Priests for Equality, 1996). And the color-coded edition of the four canonical gospels together with the *Gospel of Thomas* produced by the Jesus Seminar appears under the title *The Five Gospels: The Search for the Authentic Words of Jesus* (Polebridge Press, 1993).

~ Tools

One of the resources that will help your group begin to appreciate the rich variation in the gospel texts themselves is something called "gospel parallels"; there are a number of versions available but the classic is Burton L. Throckmorton's *Gospel Parallels: A Comparison of the Synoptic Gospels* (5th ed., Nelson, 1992). These books print the four gospels (Throckmorton omits John, but other versions do not) in parallel columns, allowing you to read horizontally, that is, with parallel content side-by-side.

I also recommend that you read an annotated Bible. The notes in them below the text bar help you traverse the terrain above, containing comments on translation decisions, contextual background, and cross-referenced citations with similar themes. The Oxford edition of the NRSV and the *HarperCollins Study Bible* are both well annotated. Roger Ferlo's volume in this series, *Opening the Bible* (Cowley, 1997), provides superb instruction on how to navigate the pages of an annotated Bible.

Other tools for reading include Bible atlases, Bible encyclopedias, and Bible dictionaries—the *Anchor Bible Dictionary* and the *Oxford Companion to the Bible* being good examples of the latter. Then there are "the commentaries," one- or two-volume tomes of detailed scholarship on single books of the Bible. These are not for the faint-hearted, and they tend to have a dry, formulaic feel. But they offer detailed verse-by-verse notes together with more discursive reflections on larger sections of related text. Commentaries often come in sets, covering—over years of publication—every book of the Bible.

If you use them, do not rely exclusively on a single series; they are always uneven. For example, my judgment is that Luke Timothy Johnson's volumes on Luke and Acts, which only recently appeared in the *Sacra Pagina* series, are the best works on these books. Raymond E. Brown's two *Anchor Bible* volumes on John, which are almost thirty years old, remain the classic commentary on that gospel. Also, avail yourself of radically divergent readings of a text. You will find, for example, that Raymond Brown's *The Birth of the Messiah* (Doubleday, 1977) and Richard Horsley's *The Liberation of Christmas* (Crossroad, 1989) treat the *Magnificat* in Luke 1:46-55 quite differently. Brown's interpretation is more or less consistent with traditional scholarship on the birth narratives, while Horsely reads with an exclusively political hermeneutic.

From time to time try dipping into the non-canonical documents that did not make it into our authorized Bibles. Many of these contain bizarre material, such as a story in the *Infancy Gospel of Thomas* where the child Jesus fashions a set of clay doves and then brings them to life. Others probably stand chronologically behind the canonical materials and have significantly informed the authors of the writings we know better. Until recently, these texts were accessible only to scholars, but the bulk of them are now available in a single volume called *The Complete Gospels* (Polebrige Press, 1992).

∼ History and Interpretation of the Bible

There are hundreds of dense and scholarly works available on biblical history and hermeneutics, but three are especially accessible to the lay reader. Robert Alter's *The Art of Biblical Narrative* (Basic Books, 1981) is a particularly imaginative approach to understanding the shape of the Hebrew scriptures. Sandra Schneiders's *The Revelatory Text* (HarperSanFrancisco, 1991) is an equally provocative and original treatment of New Testament hermeneutics. Paul Achtemeier's *The Inspiration of Scripture* (Westminster, 1980) deals clearly with both the origins of biblical literature and the differing perspectives brought to the Bible by so-called modernist and conservative readings of it. For a fourth and Anglican view on the nature of Scripture, see Frederick Borsch's *Anglicanism and the Bible* (Morehouse Barlow, 1981). Although not specifically a work on either history or hermeneutics, Peter Gomes's *The Good Book: Reading the Bible with Mind and Heart* (William Morrow, 1996) offers a refreshing look at the Bible and the ways in which we have formed our relationships to it.

Every parish Bible group I have ever taught has had dozens more questions about the origins of Christian literature—and the origins of Christianity—than I have been able to address in this work. So I recommend you consult one or more of the following for questions left unanswered. Almost any good introductory volume on the New Testament contains at least prefatory information about the origins of the Christian scriptures, but Luke Timothy Johnson's *The Writings of the New Testament* (Fortress, 1986) is among the best. A more ambitious undertaking, but no less rewarding, is Helmut Koester's two-volume *Introduction to the New Testament* (Walter de Grutyer, 1982). Also, Koester's *Ancient Christian Gospels* (Trinity, 1990), although somewhat daunting by virtue of its scholarly detail, is the most comprehensive outline of the arc of development of Christian literature from the pre-canonical texts to the canonical gospels. Perhaps more accessible is Burton Mack's *Who Wrote the New Testament?* (HarperSanFrancisco, 1995), but the reader needs to be warned that Mack, as a sociologist of religion, looks at the origins of Christian literature through the lens of social formation by way of myth-making—and does not always credit the religious experience when doing so. Still, his reconstruction of the themes and complexities of early Christian communities and their defining texts is illuminating and intriguing.

∿ The God of the Bible

A number of imaginative new looks at the God of the Bible have appeared in recent years, including Karen Armstrong's *A History of God* (Knopf, 1994) and Jack Miles's *God: A Biography* (Vantage Books, 1996). Armstrong's book tackles the God of Islam as well as the God of Christian and Hebrew scriptures, and Miles's book approaches God as a literary figure in a uniquely Hebrew narrative. Marcus Borg's *The God We Never Knew* (HarperSanFrancisco, 1997) strives to make the God of the biblical literature accessible to contemporary spirituality. Finally, for sociopolitical readings of the God of the Hebrew tradition, you may want to consult Naim Ateek's *Justice and Only Justice: A Palestinian Theology of Liberation* (Orbis Books, 1989) and Walter Brueggemann's *A Social Reading of the Old Testament* (Fortress, 1994). Both authors have significantly shaped my own view of the God of the Bible.

∿ The Jesus of the Bible

The historical Jesus project, and the Jesus Seminar in particular, have commanded so much popular attention that there is hardly a bookstore today that does not have an "historical Jesus" section. From a bewildering array of materials, I suggest a pair of books as the place to begin: *Meeting Jesus Again for the First Time* (HarperSanFrancisco, 1994) by Marcus Borg, who is among the most respected of the Jesus Seminar group, and *The Real Jesus* (HarperSanFrancisco, 1996) by Luke Timothy Johnson, who is harshly critical of the entire historical project. For more comprehensive studies of the Jesus of history, you might consult John P. Meier's two-volume work *A Marginal Jew: Rethinking the Historical Jesus* (Doubleday, 1991, 1995) and John Dominic Crossan's *The Historical Jesus: The Life of a Mediterranean Jewish Peasant* (HarperSanFrancisco, 1992). A less daunting approach to the "biography" of Jesus, one that provides the outlines but omits the extensive scholarly methodology, is Crossan's shorter volume *Jesus: A Revolutionary Biography* (HarperSanFrancisco, 1994).

Crossan's interest in the historical Jesus derives in part from his scholarly research on the passion narratives, which has become available to the lay reader in *Who Killed Jesus?* (HarperSanFrancisco, 1995). Another helpful selection is Raymond E. Brown's *A Crucified Christ in Holy Week* (Liturgical Press, 1986), which examines comparatively all four of the gospel passion narratives. Brown's larger work, *The Death of the Messiah* (Doubleday, 1994), is an exhaustive piece of scholarship on the same topic.

For a look at the cultural world through which the historical Jesus traveled, Bruce Malina's entertaining and almost cinematic *Windows on the World of Jesus: Time Travel to Ancient Judea* (Westminster, 1993) is very helpful for reading "contextually." For an examination of how Jesus has been reinterpreted in every generation, see Jaroslav Pelikan's *Jesus Through the Centuries: His Place in the History of Culture* (Harper and Row, 1985). The volume has been reissued and beautifully illustrated under the title *The Illustrated Jesus Through the Centuries* (Yale, 1997).

⁓ Feminist Studies
Feminist studies of the biblical literature has now generated its own commentary, edited by Carol A. Newsom and Sharon H. Ringe, called *The Women's Bible Commentary* (John Knox Press, 1992). The now classic work for New Testament studies is Elizabeth Schüssler-Fiorenza's *In Memory of Her: A Feminist Theological Reconstruction of Christian Origins* (Crossroad, 1983). If you are particularly interested in the feminist readings of the Bible adopted in this work—especially those related to the creation narratives discussed in chapter 5—consult both Phyllis Trible's *God and the Rhetoric of Sexuality* (Fortress, 1978) and Lisa Sowle Cahill's *Between the Sexes: Foundations for a Christian Ethics of Sexuality* (Fortress, 1985).

⁓ Reading Backward and Forward
To my knowledge, there are no authors in print who provide detailed, page-by-page assistance for the kind of approach to the Bible (or even a single book of the Bible) I suggest here—that is, reading the Bible for its past, its present, and its future. The exception is Ched Myers, who, I think, does this for the gospel of Mark and whose writings have very much influenced my own biblical reading. Over the last decade, Myers has offered a trilogy on Mark that most closely and comprehensively approximates the literal, historical, and prophetic readings I encourage you to attempt. His first volume, *Binding the Strong Man: A Political Reading of Mark's Story of Jesus* (Orbis, 1988) is an exhaustive commentary that invites the reader to look at the gospel from within the social, political, economic, cultural, and religious context of Mark's world outside his

gospel; it thus reads Mark's text for its *past*. Myers's second volume, *Who Will Roll Away the Stone? Discipleship Queries for First World Christians* (Orbis, 1994) asks the reader to move the lessons of the biblical world taught in *Binding the Strong Man* into an assessment of the modern realities of our world and the demands they make on our faith; it thus reads Mark's text for our *present*. Finally, *Say to This Mountain: Mark's Story of Discipleship* (co-authored with Marie Dennis, Joseph Nangle, Cynthia Moe-Lobeda, and Stuart Taylor; Orbis, 1996) assumes that its readers are a community of serious Bible students who are trying to integrate the Markan texts with contemporary issues so as to live the message of the gospel prophetically; thus it reads Mark's text for our *future*. Wes Howard-Brook, in *Becoming Children of God: John's Gospel and Radical Discipleship* (Orbis, 1994), attempts to do for the gospel of John what Myers has done for the gospel of Mark.

∾ A Final Note

Your study group could literally spend years working its way through the resources I have outlined here. Ched Myers's trilogy alone could occupy a triad of years. But lest you feel discouraged at the end of the Bible-reading day, my best piece of advice—and your best resource—is this: trust your own reading and your ability to voice it. When you take up the Bible to read and hear, you join in a conversation with voices like your own, other interpreters who have for centuries tried—as we do still—to appropriate the texts for their lives, moving them forward into their time and place. Some of those voices have come to be regarded more highly, more authoritatively, than others; but even so, there is no single "right" reading of the Bible. In the end, the Holy Spirit will not leave you comfortless just because your skills as a reading adept are still developing.

Questions for Group Study

In order to use this study guide, each member of the group will need an annotated Bible. In addition, the group as a whole will need a good one-volume introduction to the Bible, such as *The Oxford Companion to the Bible* or the *Jerome Bible Commentary*, as well as any of the resources suggested in the previous chapter.

∼ Prologue

The prologue sets forth this book's central theme: we come to the Bible as a community of faith seeking to discover our ancient identity as the people of God and hoping to interpret the word of God in the life of the community, both now and for the future.

1. What do you think it means to read the Bible as part of a community of faith, as opposed to reading simply for personal spiritual enlightenment? Remembering Bible study groups or sermon discussion groups of which you have been a part, what made these discussions valuable or

memorable? What made them frustrating or boring? How did they shape your understanding of Christian identity?

2. How has your experience of hearing Scripture read in the liturgy changed your understanding of the church and the meaning of its texts?

⟿ **Chapter One**
Two of the problems we encounter in the Bible are the apparent lack of sufficient historical detail and the inconsistencies between the stories told by the various writers. To some, these problems bring into question the truth of the Bible.

1. A good example of these problems is found in the story of the first Easter morning as told by Mark and Matthew. Read the story in Mark 16:1-8 and Matthew 28:1-10. What are the "facts" of the case on which the two authors agree? What is different? What might account for the similarities? Differences?

2. Now read Matthew 28:11-20. Why do you suppose these details are found in Matthew's story but in no other gospel? Now turn to Mark 16:9-20, which many believe was added to Mark's book at a later date. If so, what sources from the early church do you think might have contributed to this material? Do any of the words or phrases sound familiar? Why do you think the shorter version was expanded?

3. The author tells us that the evangelists were not afraid to change and embellish the stories they wrote down for us, just as we do when we tell and retell family stories until they are "larger than life." What examples of this expan-

sive storytelling from your own store of "family legends" have come down to you? What truths do they tell about your family?

～ Chapter Two

The most important stories in any family, community, or nation are those that tell us who we are. These stories change over the course of time as we ourselves change and reinterpret our history in the light of new experiences.

1. For Anglicans, new ways of seeing are often reflected in the prayer book and the ways it has changed over the centuries: each revision tells a different story about who we are. With this in mind, read the following passages from the 1979 American *Book of Common Prayer*, or equivalent readings from another Anglican prayer book, such as the Canadian *Book of Alternative Services.*

> Eucharistic Prayer B, "We give thanks to you, O God" (BCP 368-369)
>
> Eucharistic Prayer I, "All glory be to thee, Almighty God" (BCP 334-336)
>
> Thanksgiving Over the Water, "We thank you, Almighty God" (BCP 306-307)
>
> The Exsultet from the Great Vigil of Easter, "Rejoice now" (BCP 286-287)

What stories are we telling in each passage, and what do these stories say about who we are? If you are coming to Anglicanism from another denomination, how do these stories differ from the stories of your own tradition? If you have been raised an Anglican, how do they differ from the stories told in the church you grew up in?

2. How do the stories we tell in our prayer book liturgies reflect the stories of the Bible? How do they change or adapt those scriptural stories?

~ **Chapter Three**

With this chapter we begin to read the Bible by learning how to read for "the three senses of Scripture": the literal, the historical, and the prophetic. Turn to Luke 4:16-30, the story of Jesus in the synagogue at Nazareth. Here Jesus proclaims his message in the words of the prophet Isaiah, which allows you to explore an Old Testament text (Isaiah 61:1-2; 58:6) in the context of the gospel.

1. Read both passages first for the literal meaning, using at least two translations. Note where each passage occurs, and what precedes and follows it. (For example, the synagogue incident follows right after Jesus' temptation in the wilderness. What might that tell you?)

2. Next, look for the historical meaning, asking what both passages meant to the communities for whom they were originally written. (The prophecy from Isaiah, for example, was probably written during or just after the Babylonian exile.) Why would Jesus have used Isaiah to address the people of Nazareth?

3. Finally, discuss these texts for their prophetic meaning, in light of what they have to say to the church today.

～ Chapter Four

This chapter offers further practice in using the strategies first outlined in chapter three, and suggests a method for studying the Bible in groups. Try using the African Bible study method with the parable of the marriage feast as told by Matthew (22:1-14). In your study time, after reading the passage again, read the version of the parable told in Luke 14:16-24 and consider the historical, literal, and prophetic meanings of the texts.

1. What are the similarities and what are the differences in how the parable is told? Remember that reading "around" a text also helps with interpretation, so look also at Matthew's parable in 21:33-41 and see if you can find a theme common to both his parables.

2. Do Matthew and Luke seem to be writing for two different groups of people? Who might they be? What makes you think so? (Hint: focus particularly on the "replacement guests" in each of the two stories.)

3. How do you account for the two very different endings of the parable?

4. How would you tell a similar parable today?

～ Chapter Five

Here we will use the three senses of Scripture to explore two scriptural passages that raise ethical questions central to their time and also to our lives today, Amos 5:21-24 and 1 Corinthians 8:1-13. Although they address very different situations, both texts are outspoken on Christian responsibility toward the weak, whether in society at large or in the con-

gregation. Read for the literal, historical, and prophetic senses of each passage, and in your study time consider the following questions.

1. To whom are Amos and Paul each speaking? Would they be justified in saying something similar to us today?

2. What modern parallels to the situation in 1 Corinthians can you think of? What language might Paul and Amos use today?

～ Chapter Six

This chapter discusses the various and often contradictory aspects of God that are revealed to us throughout Scripture, from Genesis to the gospels. Here we will take two passages from the Hebrew Bible that reveal very different sides of God: Hosea 11:1-11 and Job 1:1-12.

The first passage is drawn from the book of the prophet Hosea, who was active in the kingdom of Israel during the years shortly before its conquest by the Assyrians. It is part of God's "soliloquy" on the faithlessness of Israel. The second is from the prologue to the book of Job, a well-known story in which an upright man who has been faithful to God throughout his life is suddenly deprived of everything. Read for the literal, historical, and prophetic senses of each passage and in your study time consider the following questions.

1. What do the texts tell us about justice and mercy?

2. What do they tell us about different aspects of God and God's relationship to human beings?

3. What do the texts suggest about the benefits of faithfulness?

4. How do the images of God in these texts endorse or challenge your own?

∾ **Chapter Seven**

The focus of this chapter is the figure of Jesus and the ways in which he cannot be "boxed in," nor his life reduced to a single meaning or interpretation. The multidimensional aspects of Jesus' life become clear when we compare accounts of a single incident as it is told by the different evangelists, even when the accounts are superficially very similar.

Make a close comparison of Matthew's and Luke's accounts of Jesus' teaching on the Beatitudes in Matthew 5:1-12 (part of the Sermon on the Mount) and Luke 6:20-26 (part of the Sermon on the Plain), noticing the similarities and differences between the two.

1. What do you notice about the wording of the blessings in each account? Why do you think Luke goes on to address the rich?

2. What do you think the similarities and differences reveal about the way each evangelist thinks of Jesus and his ministry?

3. What does each evangelist tell you about the demographics of "the kingdom"? Who is "in" and who is "out"? Do you think that Jesus presents a consistent picture of the kingdom from these texts? Who is inside and who is outside *your* kingdom?

~ **Chapter Eight**

This chapter discusses the Word as sacrament, a means of experiencing the reality of God through the liturgical reading of Scripture in the context of worship.

1. As you think back over the times you have heard Scripture read in church, in what ways has Scripture "taken residence" in your heart and informed the way you live out your faith? How has it affected the way you pray?

2. Reflecting on how Scripture is read in your community liturgies, do you usually experience the reading of the lessons as a time of communion with God? What hinders your hearing of Scripture in fresh and life-changing ways?

3. In what ways has the character of your particular congregation been significantly formed by its reading of Scripture or by hearing it preached?

4. In thinking and planning for its future, how does your congregation attempt to wrestle with a biblical understanding of what discipleship might look like in your community?

Cowley Publications is a ministry of the Society of St. John the Evangelist, a religious community for men in the Episcopal Church. Emerging from the Society's tradition of prayer, theological reflection, and diversity of mission, the press is centered in the rich heritage of the Anglican Communion.

Cowley Publications seeks to provide books, audio cassettes, and other resources for the ongoing theological exploration and spiritual development of the Episcopal Church and others in the body of Christ. To this end, it is dedicated to developing a new generation of theological writers, encouraging them to produce timely, creative, and stimulating publications of excellence, and making these publications available widely, reaching both clergy and lay persons.